Kouros nestled in pink cistus and bergenia at Dyffryn Fernant.

Discovering Welsh Gardens

20 of the liveliest gardens selected
and explored by Stephen Anderton
and photographed by Charles Hawes.

Topiary garden, Nant-yr-Eryd.

GRAFFEG

contents

'somewhere beautiful'

Since you have bought this book and are, I imagine, as fascinated and thrilled by gardens as I am, you will know that today we live in a Golden Age of gardens. We have never had it so good. Since the 1980s historic gardens, public and private, from the 17th to the 20th century, have been revitalised and now run in remarkably good order. Thousands of domestic gardens good and bad lovingly open their gates, and there you can find everything from romantic cottage gardening to fashion-conscious urban Minimalism to raging kitsch, from ecologically-minded meadow gardening to fruit and vegetables and sometimes to hilarious bad taste. Gardening has never been so popular.

But hang on: England is the place the world associates with gardens. Percy Grainger and his horticultural ditty have a lot to answer for. What about the gardens of Wales? Are there any? Ask a garden-savvy American and he might say, 'Well, Powis Castle, Bodnant...' and there the words would dry up. Many an English or Scottish gardener would give you the same answer, adding, perhaps, that the cold winds from Wales were a terrible nuisance. These answers come from ignorance. True, in Wales good gardens are nowhere near as thick on the ground as they are in Kent and Sussex, but they are there, and of every kind. It's time somebody wrote about them. Now this book is not intended to be a treatise on Welsh garden history; in most historic gardens you can buy a guidebook which puts the garden in its historical context. Nor is it a comprehensive gazetteer to every Welsh garden large and small, although the important gardens are listed at the back of the book, in groups convenient for visiting. Instead, I want to show you what is happening in a cross-section of lively Welsh gardens, to present a picture of how Welsh gardens tick, now.

There have been periods when Welsh gardens actually helped to set the fashion for gardens throughout Britain. At the end of the 18th century the Picturesque movement promoted landscape gardens less smooth and serene than those of Capability Brown, landscapes that were rougher, wilder, more varied, and offered carefully contrived set-piece views. Not surprisingly, the rugged Welsh landscape offered wonderful opportunities for this kind of 'picture'. Hafod, near Aberystwyth, was an extraordinarily influential Picturesque landscape and its gushing ravines and bridges can still be found under a smothering of commercial forestry. Piercefield, outside Chepstow, was a fine Picturesque landscape, whose walks overlooking the Wye Valley and Chepstow can still be appreciated from the footpaths behind the racecourse. In 1782, William Gilpin's *Observations on the River Wye and Several Parts of South Wales* made the ruined Tintern Abbey, in the Wye Valley, one of the great icons of the Picturesque.

Wales has always been border country and a militarily troubled landscape. In the 13th century, King Edward I built his series of fortress castles around Wales, to establish conspicuous control over a subjugate population. Many were later wrecked in battle, or rendered indefensible by the might of Oliver Cromwell so the Welsh could not use them for their own defence. Some Welsh castles, ironically, were finally tamed by becoming civilised mansions with gardens; Chirk Castle is a fine example. Powis Castle's famous tropical flower borders sit upon a series of elegant seventeenth-century terrace gardens. Raglan Castle, ruinated but not razed to the ground, was once a fine Renaissance palace with a garden that was perhaps the most ambitious of its time in Wales.

But castles do not have the monopoly on ruins: many a Welsh cottage still has old or ruined outbuildings which are today being incorporated into the garden, as places to sit or as shady ferneries. How the Picturesque movement would have approved! Cottage gardening, whether for produce or ornament, has always been a part of Welsh gardening, and on the drovers' roads through the Black Mountains where I live it is still possible to find box bushes twice as tall as the ruined cottages in whose gardens they once were planted, telling the tale of gardens gone by.

For some people, Wales conjures images of mining valleys and shipyards, and its very mention provokes smart remarks about rain and sheep; but industry only ever covered a small part of Wales, and by English standards it is mostly unspoilt countryside

with a mercifully low population (the sheep, I admit, we do have aplenty, and if it rains a lot in some parts of west Wales, well so it does in Cumbria, and gardeners in the increasingly parched south east England are already jealous of an even half-generous rainfall). Unspoilt countryside means that many a gardener today, just like the landed gentry of the 18th century, can have the pleasure and face the discipline of relating a garden to its surrounding countryside. One person might use a distant snow-topped mountain as the focus for a vista; another might attempt to plant a seamless transition from garden to the wild landscape. With landscapes as appealing as theirs, how could anyone resist incorporating them into a garden? Yet fine inward-looking gardens are being made in Wales too. In suburban Swansea is a modern formal garden that ranks amongst the best in Britain, shutting out its surroundings to create a secluded, cool, green world. Near Chepstow is a series of underground grottoes fit for a horticulturally-minded demon king. There are thoughtful, modern gardens too: one belongs to the photographer whose wonderful pictures fill this book, and which I make no bones about rating one of the best in Wales.

Who has made Wales's great gardens? It's the same mixture of types as anywhere else: the great British designers of the past from Brown and Repton to Nesfield, and then others like William Eames and Henry Avray Tipping who had a particular impact on Wales; gentleman amateurs like John Price at Plas Cadnant, or aristocrats like Thomas Johnes at Hafod and the McLaren family at Bodnant doing their own grand thing; obsessives, plantaholics, nurserymen with a more artistic eye and as ever – dare I say it – not a few expat Europeans and English, amongst whom I must number myself, who want somewhere only lightly developed and populated in which to garden. Somewhere beautiful.

Every garden is an expression of its makers' character and each one has the power to thrill and provoke people in different ways; that is what gardens are for. Heaven protect us from gardens that are merely soothing, when they can be exciting as well: on the railway line to horticultural heaven, soothing is often only a few stops short of boring. As you read this book and I hope one day visit the gardens, you must decide for yourself what these gardens do best and what they do badly and how you would improve them. Use an enquiring, critical and imaginative eye, because no garden is immune to the imaginative process and the prospect of change; even the plants themselves, the lifeblood of gardens, are always growing and decaying and the picture always changing. That is their greatest flaw and our greatest pleasure.

Charles Hawes and I both came to live in Wales to make gardens, I much more recently than he, and it was seeing his garden at The Veddw that first made me want more seriously to explore gardens in Wales. He is a friend as well as my collaborator on this book and we have worked and travelled together for many other projects and publications.

It is our habit always to discuss vigorously the gardens we see, to consider what we do and don't like, what seems to work and what does not, and so this book is the result of such deliberations, albeit that the thoughts and opinions expressed in the text are, for better or worse, mine; we often disagree and he'll have to lump it if he does. On the other hand, I could not take such wonderful photographs. They are the result of weeks on the road and much dedication rising at 5am to catch the morning light; a garden photographer's life was never a cushy number.

Stephen Anderton
Abergavenny

Aberglasney

Tywi Valley, south west Wales

'this plain garden has been brought back to life, like an old Quaker dress salvaged from a trunk'

Candelabra primulas, hostas and rodgersias.

Gardens live perpetually on the slippery slope to jungle. Only cut the maintenance, cut the investment, cut the care, and down they go, far faster than you'd expect. After 500 years of ups and downs Aberglasney in 1995 was truly a mess. Twenty years of neglect had brought it to dereliction and it was only saved from ruin through the energies of a dedicated band of individuals. It is now open to the public.

Gardens are restored for a variety of reasons: a garden might be a superb example of a particular style or designer's work, it might have political, literary or historical associations, or contain a remarkable collection of plants. Aberglasney was something especially rare – a fine example of a mid-seventeenth-century garden on not too grand a scale.

What lingers in the mind after a visit are the garden's monumental walls. It's perhaps their sheer substance that preserved them from the destructive power of fashion. So many a garden of this age has had its structure smoothed away by the landscape gardeners of the eighteenth-century, but here in mid Wales, where the lust for fashionability was less voracious, the bones of the seventeenth-century garden were tolerated and broadly-speaking survived, except for the overlaying of a Victorian terrace below the house.

Walls define the entire garden, creating a series of enclosures – two productive walled gardens, a formal courtyard garden, and a rectangular pool garden. Most striking and memorable is the broad terrace walk raised on a cloistered arcade, which looks out over the pool to the countryside beyond. Yet it's no grand prospect, just a few foreground woods and fields, a further reinforcement of the modest, comfortable atmosphere of Aberglasney.

Opposite: **Simple rhythms, of castellated walls, of clipped box, of the light and shade under the cloisters, help to give Aberglasney its charm.**

Above: **The pool garden with its weeping ash but minus its island.**

The cloister garden laid out in a manner typical of the 1600s, with orange trees and simple grass plats.

The cloister garden was the subject of serious but inconclusive garden archaeology and now shows a layout fashionable in the early 1600s: simple grass plats, orange trees in tubs and period roses.

The first of the walled kitchen gardens has stayed true to its original purposes also, and contains apples, pears and apricots beautifully trained on the walls, a tunnel of crab apples, and straight rows of vegetables and flowers for cutting.

The productive walled garden with Lavender 'Munstead' and purple Celosia.

The second walled garden has been given a freer treatment. No rows of vegetables here but a new formal flower garden designed by Penelope Hobhouse. The design is simple enough, which is important in a garden so uncomplicated overall. Two concentric rings of beds lie at the centre of the walled rectangle, punctuated by yew cones and approached by cruciform paths. Within the beds are rich plantings of perennials especially good in late season and all the better for being visible from the terrace above, where cherries and strawberries grow in the restored pheasant-rearing

cages. It is only a shame that, since the walled garden slopes in two directions at once, Hobhouse's formal, geometric pattern sits somewhat inelegantly in its space, and the complication of further new beds around the perimeter walls will not reduce the effect.

Simplicity is Aberglasney's greatest asset, and to that same end the removal of a fussy little island from the pool has done wonders to calm a scene already busy with a café, a glasshouse and holiday cottages behind.

The walled garden designed by Penelope Hobhouse. Plenty of summer colour but also strong evergreen bones for winter.

Today all gardens have to earn their keep and often that means extending the period of plant interest. Here this has meant adding two informal woodland gardens, one of them on the site of a former 18th century collection of American woodland trees. The streamsides are planted with swathes of magenta primulas and blue poppies, and amongst the trees are magnolias, sweet witch hazels and rhododendrons.

Aberglasney, then, is far from a strict historic recreation. The approach has been freer, partly for lack of precise planting records (sometimes a blessed release) and partly for the wish to let the garden live a life of its own, now, with modern planting and new developments on a not inappropriate scale. Curious, perhaps, that, while the garden is keen to flag up its original features and even the changes made by subsequent generations, it does not say more of the present admirable policy to develop the garden's planting.

'streamsides planted with swathes of primulas and blue poppies'

Above and opposite: **Candelabra primulas luxuriate and self-sow beside water, with the leathery fern Blechnum chilense.**

Left: **Hosta sieboldiana with the ostrich fern, Matteucia struthiopteris, and the pale plumes of Rodgersia aesculifolia.**

Sad to say, the house is largely empty and some of it still a shell, which never makes people warm to a garden. Fortunately, some of the unroofed space to the rear of the house was given a glass roof in 2005, to allow warm temperate and sub-tropical plants to grow amongst the bare walls – palms, gingers, orchids and rare magnolias new to science. It is called the Ninfarium after the famous garden, Ninfa, outside Rome, which was made upon the impossibly romantic ruins of a town sacked in the 14th century. In reality the Ninfarium, because of its drier indoor atmosphere, is almost clinical by comparison. One longs for an explosion of yogurt to encourage mosses floor to ceiling and a Latin rush of the Ninfa magic. Still, on a winter's day in Wales it is quite a surprise.

That coolness of atmosphere is integral to the attraction of Aberglasney: the empty pond, the tunnel of gnarled yews, the stone gatehouse standing alone, those wonderful walls. It is so good that this plain garden has been brought back to life, like an old Quaker dress salvaged from a trunk, and the fact that it has been done by a private trust, not government, one which has had to coax and cajole for every penny it has spent, is hugely to its credit. But at present that dress, after all its restoration, feels freshly laundered, newly back from the cleaners. Now it needs to relax a little, become comfortable again as the planting matures; but the fuss of the new development needs to stay separate outside the walls. No sequins on the dress itself. Let it stay cool.

Bananas in the Ninfarium.

Left: **Ferns and cycads at home in the Ninfarium.**

Below left: **The gatehouse.**

Below: **Gnarled trunks in the yew tunnel.**

Bodnant

Conwy, north Wales

'its 80 acres take full advantage of dramatic views west to Snowdonia and of the opportunity to grow an extraordinary range of plants'

Pampas grass at its best on the lily pool terrace.

'this is the grand manner indeed'

Bodnant is one of the great gardens of Wales. Its 80 acres take full advantage of the dramatic views west to Snowdonia and of the opportunity to grow an extraordinary range of plants. Its grandest move was the construction in 1904 –1914 of a descending series of wide terraces that push out from the house fully 200 metres into the valley. This is the grand manner indeed, to be compared with the Victorian terraces at Harewood House and Waddesdon Manor. Bodnant bears all its trophies on this west side: the terraces, the stupendous view to the mountains and, out of sight down below, the woodland valley garden, known as the dell. Bodnant Hall is neither elegant nor pretty nor romantic (heavy-duty sandstone and blue granite topped with mock-Tudor gables, there's a whiff of nursing home) but from its ledge on the side of the valley it commands its garden perfectly.

The hall was built for Henry Pochin and it was he who planted the newly introduced exotic conifers which so dominate the dell today. Pochin's daughter Laura, a keen gardener herself, married Charles McLaren, later to become the first Lord Aberconway, and she brought up their son Henry to take over the garden in due course. It was Henry, the second Lord Aberconway who, until his death in 1953, created the terraces and much of Bodnant as we see it today. It was he, too, who gave the garden to the National Trust in 1949, although the family continued to manage and develop it. Henry was succeeded by his son Charles who died in 2000 and, like his father, was for a time President of the Royal Horticultural Society.

People new to Bodnant invariably arrive wanting to see the famous laburnum tunnel, dripping yellow in June, but surprisingly it's just a peripheral feature squeezed rather ashamedly up in a corner by the road. First to be seen on arrival is a long mixed border against a tall wall covered in climbers, which clearly sets out the garden's ambitions to plantsmanship.

Then instead of taking the obvious route ahead to the top terrace and the real start of the garden, the inevitable 'Private' sign heads you off into rather institutional informal lawns, shrubberies and specimen flowering trees, through which you must sidle to the terraces. Not that there aren't wonderful distractions along the way: there are magnolias galore, a superb old chestnut on a plinth of moss, and a vast oak standing sentinel to the view into a pretty little parkland, of ridges, hummocks and copses set in a golden sea of meadow grass.

Top: **Laburnum tunnel.**

Right: **Magnolia time beside the house.**

Far right: **A fine, focal oak with the ha-ha and park beyond.**

And already the famous rhododendrons have begun. Bodnant has long been a great breeding centre for rhododendrons and the entire garden is full of them, as well as all those other coveted woodland flowering plants: camellias, azaleas, eucryphias, magnolias, Japanese maples, dogwoods – the list is endless and the autumn colour terrific. It is one of the great showcases of Britain. On the other hand, you might say the garden does not know where to call a halt to its winding woodland paths and shrubberies. But then, even after National Trust ownership, Bodnant remained very firmly a personal Aberconway preserve, and the National Trust's gardens advisers were tolerated rather than heeded. Since the death of the 3rd Lord Aberconway in 2000 there has been a more cooperative partnership.

The marvel of Bodnant's terraces is that they are deep enough to seem like a series of separate gardens in their own right, not just a series of landings from which to admire the distant mountains. The famous pin mill terrace, named for the pretty building moved here from Worcestershire, is boldly centred on a grand canal that runs side to side across its terrace; it is wrapped with trees and largely ignores the view.

Opposite page: **The blue cedars are beautiful but suffering now from old age. Scarlet embothrium in full fling. The delights of autumn.** Above: **The Pin Mill.**

The terraces are Bodnant's focus of summer colour, their flower-laden formality following on from the dell's woodland fireworks in spring. By the 1990s much of the garden around the house, terraces included, had begun to get stale. Old and out-of-scale trees were no longer being removed and replaced, worn-out old rose beds lingered on for sentimental reasons, and it was becoming an old man's garden. Since 2000 there have been real changes and the garden is back in gear. Tired or diseased plantings are being taken out, whole hedge systems dug out and replaced, borders replanted, wall-trained shrubs taken in hand again, and overhanging trees cut back. It is getting the much needed makeover of a lifetime.

Above: **Achillea and dahlias.**

Right: **The green theatre, decrepit, but still looking good from a distance. It has been ripped out and replanted.**

A new planting of roses on the terraces still struggles to soften the heavy-duty paving.

Exotic conifers rise from lawn in the dell, much more Gardenesque than Picturesque.

Down below all this is that delightfully strange beast, the dell. The prospect of a steep, rocky valley running down to a rushing river sounds Picturesque enough, but actually it is heavily gardened; a fairytale, dingley dell, not a rugged, wild garden, even if it is on a large scale. Along the valley floor the winding Hiraethlyn, hardly a river, is flanked by bright blue hydrangeas for summer, and earlier by swathes of waterside perennials. Little bridges let the path swap sides.

Perhaps the most telling aspect of the dell is that the valley floor is not wild but a perfect green lawn studded with towering redwoods and firs, and divided by politely sinuous paths. It's like a child's painting of a garden, a Gardenesque, Victorian fantasy in the best public parks manner (nothing wrong with that) and of course, packed with wonderful plants.

The elegantly solid old mill building by the river is the focus of the dell, the place where visitors first arrive at the valley floor. There is a touch of the kiosk developing here, with potted evergreens and fashionable tree ferns, as if a spoonful of suburbia had landed in the valley bottom. But as you walk up the valley to the lake it is quickly left behind, and the sight of the family mausoleum perched high on the valley's rim is thoroughly romantic; more Valhalla than crematorium.

The dell in romantic mode.

Bodrhyddan

Denbighshire, north Wales

'swirling parterres with slabs of begonias in no-nonsense red, pink and white – the faint-hearted should put on their sunglasses'

Begonia semperflorens in Nesfield's muscular parterre.

What a surprise is Bodrhyddan. When you hear a house has been in the same family for ever and a day, in this case the Rowley-Conwys, you imagine sober, sleepy ranges of honey-coloured stone where time has stood still and probably always will. But here you drive up to the main house – what a treat to turn at the front door for once – and there it is, a tall, rollicking, frolicking red brick and stone confection of a house that you might expect to see in Knightsbridge rather than Denbighshire. It was built for the then Lord Langford in 1875 by William Eden Nesfield, in Cadogan Square-style. You have to smile.

Go round the side of the house and you will smile again, for here is an extraordinary parterre, designed by William Andrews Nesfield, father of William Eden and, along with Sir Charles Barry (who built the Houses of Parliament), one of the great nineteenth-century designers of parterres. W. A. Nesfield had a major hand in designing both Green Park and Kew.

Now Nesfield usually liked his swirling parterres to be intricate, often with tiny box hedges only inches high, and with areas of coloured glass and gravels in between. What you see here is far more muscular. Knee-high box hedges surround day-glow slabs of begonias in no-nonsense red, pink and white. The faint-hearted should put on their sunglasses. You may hate it or you may love it, but there is no denying the vigour and high quality of the work. See how the soil in the beds is mounded up from decades of composting.

'like Guardsmen holding their swords
over a bride at a wedding'

It's not a parterre in which to stroll, however. If you come out of the house's central door there is actually no direct entrance to the path system, it is rolled out there to be seen head-on, a big, naïve rug of a parterre for a minor country house, unlike the more elegant, intricate parterres to be seen at palaces like Harewood in Yorkshire or Waddesdon in Buckinghamshire, in which there is space for people to circulate amongst the beds, often on grass, and to admire the planting.

The Bodrhyddan parterre is not impregnable, however; halfway down a path runs across, past a fountain, and it's approached by pairs of drum-shaped yews, some of them bridged at the top like guardsmen holding their swords over a bride at a wedding. You expect confetti. And in between the yew drums are single standard red roses which, had the gardener time enough and a Playing Card costume, she might paint white in Alice in Wonderland style. It is all great fun.

It's also pretty unfashionable. Look at the monster parterre by Barry at Trentham Hall in Staffordshire, now beautifully planted by Tom Stuart Smith with grasses and mixed perennials, and you see how stolid Bodrhyddan looks, even if the colours are vibrant. But its old-fashionedness is part of its charm. We are at Rhyl here, not just off the M6, and things move more slowly; it's this pace of change that allows us still to see a garden like this, to enjoy how different it is. Ironically, during the 1939-1945 war the parterre was planted with vegetables – a 1980s potager before its time.

Left: **Pairs of clipped yew march towards the centre of the parterre.**

Bodrhyddan's entrance drive runs through a young avenue of limes which sets the tone for the garden; this is a place where trees of age and dignity are valued and cared for; in the Pleasance for example, a few acres of ornamental woodland in the best Victorian, Gardenesque style, which has been dragged back from a bramble jungle since 1983. In here is St Mary's Well, the spring which was the likely cause for the house being built on this spot in the first place, and it is capped with a little well-house of 1612; but this architectural lollipop pales into insignificance compared to the surrounding trees.

There are superb old oaks and sycamores, and a grove of redwoods. Most of the deciduous trees have had their lower branches cut away for some considerable way, letting in sufficient light for lawn to grow beneath them, and it's made soft with moss and mind-your-own-business. The occasional box bush has been clipped to make a mound (some too dinky by half), but the roundness of the bigger shapes, the verticals of the trunks, and the play of light and shadow upon the grass combine to make a magical effect. Just green plains and lines and curves and volumes, and the perfect antidote to that rip-roaring parterre.

The clean trunks and clipped shapes of the Pleasance have the amiable feel of a public park.

A rustic cobbled path runs under the trees to the end of the woodland, laid down as a Japanese Walk of Life in the 1870s. At the end is a rockery bank fringed with flower borders, crude work by modern standards, on top of which is a temple summerhouse, built in 2000. Below it, from a terrace decked with pots of terracotta and plastic, gushes a noisy little waterfall. Everything is wonderfully domestic and unsophisticated. In the summerhouse are plastic loungers and a ghetto-blaster; outside bird-feeders and wind chimes dangle from the trees, and shrubs which ought not to be clipped in order to flower properly, are clipped. The left-over begonias from the parterre are used to fill up gaps in the rockery borders and (a modern touch) the view down to the pond behind the summerhouse is topped with a waving sea of grasses – Stipa tenuissima and arundinacea. Their rising silvery wisps set against the sage green blanket weed on the pond, with the branches of a weeping willow scoring down behind, make an arresting composition of greens.

You might say the Pleasance looks like a public park and indeed it has that flavour of the great Victorian gardens which reached its most popular incarnation in early twentieth-century parks. But at Bodrhyddan it is domesticated, humanised, and an absolute delight.

Far left: **The summerhouse of 2000.**

Left: **Objet trouvé planté.**

Bodysgallen

Llandudno, north Wales

'one of the best, most ambitious, characterful and delightful hotel gardens one could find anywhere'

Valerian grows from a garden wall above the parterre.

The garden at Bodysgallen is rather special. The house is at its core a thirteenth-century watch tower for Conwy Castle, but it has been regularly added to over the centuries. Now a sober amalgam of accretions from several centuries, it looks down upon a garden which also possesses features from several centuries. Most rare of these, if not the most glamorous, is a long seventeenth-century terrace, from which to view Conwy Castle at its river mouth and Snowdonia in the far distance.

Bodysgallen is also remarkable in that it is both a hotel and has a genuinely cherished, hardworking garden. Historic House Hotels bought Bodysgallen in a parlous state in 1980 and spent several years bringing both the house and the garden into a fit state. It was to be the first of three historic houses converted into hotels by the company, and one can only praise the company for putting so much money effort into their gardens. It might be said that they should never have bought the places if they were not going to keep them up, but that is unfortunately not the way of the world, and in this case the hotel has gone on to make developments to the garden which far surpass the call of duty.

Much of the structure of the garden today dates from the late 19th and early 20th century. Until then the great L-shaped area of sunken land below the house was in all likelihood just an orchard. After the Second World War the house ran as a tourist attraction for a time, until finally in 1967 the owners, the Mostyn Estate, sold up. It then became an eccentrically-managed guesthouse, before passing into the present company's hands in 1980.

'geometry best appreciated from above'

The whole of the formal garden can be seen from the terrace close under the house walls, where an Edwardian pond sits flanked by domes of golden yew and on a rocky wall the spiny, succulent rosettes of Agave americana have survived undamaged for many years now. But most striking, from these upper levels, is to look down upon the box parterre set out in a walled garden below, its geometry best appreciated from above, as it is in the great parterres at Pitmedden and Dunrobin in Scotland.

The origins of the Bodysgallen parterre are uncertain. It may well date from the late 16th century; there was certainly a parterre here in the 1790s, and it appears to have been replanted around 1900. When the hotel took over the parterre was riddled with ground elder, now largely eradicated, and the hedges had grown to such a width that the paths between them had closed up. Today the hedges are crisp and clean again, and many of the spaces between are filled with herbs including lavender, sage, rue and grey santolina.

'Lady Augusta's rose garden began life in 1904'

The walled rose garden, spread out below the terrace, is the largest and in some ways the weakest of the garden's features. It began life in 1904 as a scheme for Lady Augusta Mostyn, and remains very similar to this day. The garden is quartered by simple cruciform paths centred on a well and lined either side by clipped box or standard roses; geometric rose beds stand at the centre of each grass quadrant (there may have been a tennis court in here too), and flower borders line the perimeter walls. It is simple to the point of blankness and barely strong enough to command the open space, although domes of topiarised silver pear bring a little more substance. The roses themselves, all white, which ought to be the glory of the place, are a disaster, feeble from having grown in the same place for too long; time to ring the changes now, 'Lady Augusta's rose garden' or not. Getting some pizzazz into this space would lift the pace of the entire garden.

An overgrown bank of yews nearby has been cleared to form a fruit and vegetable garden and a classical gazebo built to face back to the house is the first inkling that there is more garden to come. A path now winds onwards through woodland carpeted with snowdrops to the seventeenth-century grass terrace, which sits along the lip of the hill overlooking Conwy. Today it is an entirely informal affair, but still its views are powerful, even if the middle ground has been subject to some housing development. Thank goodness for the trees in the foreground which do a good job editing the prospect. The hotel has in fact bought 220 acres of surrounding land in order to be less at the mercy of encroaching development; it now has the visual insulation that all good gardens need, as well as its maintenance obligations.

Wineberries, artichokes and beautifully clipped box – so much attention for just a minor path.

An example of the hotel's investment in the garden is a sham castle, of stone, built on a hillock near the terrace as an eye-catcher. Granted, it's tiny compared to those of the great eighteenth-century landscape gardens like Hagley Hall, nor is it even as large as the 1915 sham castle at Plas Brondanw, but it serves exactly the same purpose: to be seen from the house and other vantage points, and be to a place from which to see the next designed view.

To this end the hotel built a stone obelisk in 1993. How many hotels build their own 64ft obelisks? The obelisk is a fine advertisement for the hotel to those driving along the main road to Llandudno and it can be seen on its ridge from many a surrounding hill. But more importantly it keeps alive the tradition of landscape gardening, of thinking big, of being prepared to spend serious money on the features of a garden. A hotel will always have commercial priorities that may not coincide with those of its garden. It may be more important sometimes to have the front lawns immaculate at the expense of the woodland work, and that is understandable. But Bodysgallen is still one of the best, most ambitious, characterful and delightful hotel gardens one could find anywhere. It is alive.

The sham castle and 64ft obelisk.

Cae Hir

Ceredigion, west Wales

'the garden is at an interesting point in its life; if it was human we would say it is of a certain age'

Most of the garden ornament is in rusted steel.

'this is a collector's garden if ever there was'

Cae Hir is a long way from anywhere: you might call it a vast 1970s-1980s Home Counties garden set down in deepest west Wales. And the most curious thing about it is that it has been made not by another Englishman moving to a beautiful landscape and fecund climate, but by a Dutchman, Will Akkermans.

Akkermans came to Wales in 1983 at the age of forty, escaping life as a French teacher in the Netherlands. He and his wife house-hunted with a spade, testing the soil wherever they went and finally settling upon Cae Hir – the Long Field – with its four acres of rough grazing behind the cottage and two more, boggier acres, below the road on which the cottage stands. The top of the garden is 200ft higher than the stream

at the bottom, and it rains frequently and generously upon the sandy loam.

When an experienced gardener enters Cae Hir bells ring, and so they should; for Akkermans, son of a family of nurserymen, had a seminal revelation when he was visiting the Royal Horticultural Society's garden at Wisley, in Surrey. "I saw them making money from that," he says with a glow, "and I thought I can do that!"and so he did. He made a plan for the whole garden very much in the manner of Wisley (or Harlow Carr, Great Comp or Holehird) and he prepared the land. Planting started in 1985 with a lorry load of very miscellaneous trees and shrubs sent over by his brothers, and three years later he opened to the public. This is a collector's garden if ever

there was, and yet Akkermans does not think of himself as a plantsman. "I am a picture-maker" he says, and in a sense he's right: he is making a picture of a typical late twentieth-century garden. Wisley was his inspiration and he was never a regular visitor to other gardens; today he is too busy to visit other gardens because, quite remarkably, he manages Cae Hir on his own.

Opposite: **Sweeping, shrub-girt, open lawns with specimen trees form the narrative of the garden.**

Below left: **Every inch is planted and the paths fit exactly a ride-on mower.**

Below: **A fine eucalyptus leans down its trunks.**

Wisley of course is an institution, which
people either love or love to hate, whereas
Cae Hir is most definitely a private garden.
A Wisley with a heart. Yes, it has the same
flowing, open lawns bounded by continents
of trees, shrubs and perennials, and yes,
fine specimen trees also stand like islands
upon the sward.

Top: **Spikes of pale pink Persicaria bistorta surround a long seat high in the garden.**

Above right: **The red flowers of Euphorbia griffithii always attract attention.**

But it is the many separate, un-Wisley enclosures which give the garden its own quirky personality and attraction. One is a little hedged and gravelled rectangle in dappled shade, where bonsai stand on the ground or on plinths, in simple bowls and troughs. These are not posh or ancient bonsai but bonsai made simply to see what trees will do when kept small. The trees are seedlings of trees and shrubs from the garden – a hazel, conker, thorn or a pear, occasionally two plants in one bowl. There's a little greenhouse of cacti nearby, into which visitors can wander if they wish.

Top: **Bonsai on parade.**

Right: **Purple Geranium x magnificum.**

Opposite: **Clumps of Crocosmia sweep down to the house.**

Towards the top of the garden is a seat enclosed by a 30-yard semicircle of laburnums. What a sight it is, and such a change from the inevitable laburnum pergola made in homage to Bodnant or Barnsley House. Each laburnum at Cae Hir is seed-grown and multi-stemmed too, to stop the arrangement looking too rigid or sophisticated in a garden where there are soft rolling hills just a step away. Akkermans's colour-themed enclosures are more of an acquired taste. One of them, the yellow garden, consists almost entirely of clipped or unclipped conifers – yews, cypresses and thujas – with heathers, alchemilla and golden crocosmias below. It is a palette of possibilities more than a restful picture. The purple garden is equally confrontational: a ring of purple Norway maples surrounds a second ring of tall purple berberis hedges which surrounds a third ring of pink geraniums, paeonies and shrub roses. Within this is a circular path and, at its epicentre, is a great drum of purple berberis. It's like wearing purple-tinted glasses. The cooler, grey-blue garden is a little formal allée of cypress, eucalyptus, hebe, spruce and rhododendron, where a battle between shade-creating and sun-loving species has got beyond the first skirmishes.

Opposite: **The gentle landscape seen from the top of the garden.**

Above: **The yellow garden, with pompom Cupressus macrocarpa 'Goldcrest'.**

Left: **Berberis arch leading to the Purple Garden.**

The garden across the road seems not dissimilar in character at first, with more large beds of trees, shrubs and perennials. But the beds here are ringed with low hedges to create a little crispness, since Akkermans has never intended to practise such close maintenance on this side of the road. Again there are formal moments: a metal gazebo with a framework sheathed in tight-cropped golden ivy, a rectangular raised bed carpeted by sedum and

interrupted only by a dolmen of slate. But then comes a series of naturalistic lily ponds and, finally, a beautiful, fast-flowing alder stream overhung with pale rambler roses and framing views out to sheep in a valley-bottom pasture. Horticulture in the face of agriculture.

Cae Hir is a great lesson in what thrives in cool wet conditions. Trees and conifers grow like the clappers, and Akkermans

makes the most of stalwart, self-sufficient, untrendy plants that also thrive in Scotland and Northern England but are frequently shunned in south east England: Inula hookeri, Buddleia globosa, yellow loosestrife, Lilium pyrenaicum, Pilosella aurantiaca and a gamut of the most muscle-bound hardy geraniums.

The blue garden from outside, with eucalyptus, blue spruce and cypress hedges.

Cae Hir is at an interesting point in its life; if it was human we would say it is 'of a certain age'. The first trees are maturing, especially the conifers, and even more vigorous thinning must happen now, lest a great deal of the varied shrub and perennial planting should disappear under a wood of exotic trees. Decisions, decisions, decisions. Do you save the tree before the shrub, or shrub before the tree? Perhaps Akkermans, at 66, will have the energy to see it through.

Perhaps his children really will take over and get the tea-room into action. Whatever Cae Hir's future, you have to admire the place: it is brave, busy, intriguing, full of good plants and totally unexpected in west Wales.

Below the road, a dolmen standing in a sea of sedum leads down to the ponds and stream.

Dewstow

Monmouthshire, south Wales

'nothing is sophisticated and yet everything
is done with great love and earnest theatricality'

**A subterranean Victorian fantasy from
the early 20th century.**

It seems appropriate that from the garden at Dewstow you can see the massive Severn bridges because there is definitely a seaside air about the place. It's a fat lady in a booth sort of place, a winter gardens where pink and white ice-cream cones would not come amiss. Yet at the same time Dewstow is an astonishing piece of horticulture and history and engineering; it just happens to be fun as well, and those who choose to be sniffy about Dewstow do so to their own loss. It's a delight, and far better than its advertising might suggest.

Dewstow Hidden Gardens and Grottoes began life simply as Dewstow House. The garden was developed between 1893 and 1940 by Henry Oakley, a wealthy 'bachelor' who left his estate to his solicitor, who turned out, post mortem, to be Oakley's illegitimate son. How tidy. Oakley's other passion was horticulture and he employed the firm of Pulham & Son to lay out his garden, perhaps taking his stylistic cue from the garden of fellow fern-lover E.J. Lowe at nearby Shirenewton Hall. The Pulhams' speciality was hugely-skilful artificial rockwork made from specialised cements over a rubble core; for Oakley, they created pools and ravines above ground and, below, a series of top-lit tunnels and caverns. The caverns have the flavour of those at Hawkstone Hall in Shropshire, a Picturesque landscape garden of precipitous cliff-top walks made in the 1790s and culminating in a fabulous series of rocky tunnels and caverns. Dewstow is Hawkstone's jolly little grandson, thoroughly Gardenesque but tarred with the brush of the Picturesque.

The fact that Dewstow is on show today is largely due to the efforts of one man, John Harris, a local farmer who bought Dewstow House and its land to tidy up a hole in his estate (he is diversifying into golf courses). Harris still lives with his family in Dewstow House, a modest gentleman's residence with a pillared verandah, hanging baskets and plastic double glazing.

When Harris arrived, Oakley's garden was literally buried. Previous owners had filled in the pools and the entrances to the underground cavern system and it was only the discovery, while gardening, of inexplicable chunks of rockwork that caused the garden to be excavated. Little by little, and with no public finance, Harris has been clearing the pools, opening up the caverns and replanting. He's a farmer, he gets on with things.

In Oakley's day one might have entered the garden and caves by heading out of the front door and visiting his long-gone range of lean-to conservatories. The alternative – to enter the cave system from the tunnel in the cellar – is perhaps not what Harris wants now the garden is open to the public; images of Toad Hall and weasel invasions come to mind. For visitors today, therefore, the garden has a curious lack of narrative, no particular start and finish, and this encourages the idea that it is merely a series of amusements.

Opposite top: **The garden looks down to the river Severn and its great bridges.**

Opposite below: **Dewstow House.**

Left: **Once a conservatory, now an outdoor border.**

The pond has been dredged and a modern pump installed.

Foreground left: **The long panicles of Hydrangea quercifolia.**

Above: **Tomb-like entrance to the pump house, seen across the swimming pond.**

Right: **The little square formal garden, tucked amongst the trees.**

The pools, with their waterfall and fountain, meander across the front of the house, separated by grassy hollows, sweeps of perennials and a bog garden. The planting is modern and highly unsophisticated, but eminently suitable to the Gardenesque, Oakley style. One pool was originally a swimming pond and another for ducks. Nearby is a curious, sunny little formal garden right alongside an open-topped rockwork grotto with a pool at its centre. There is something charmingly zoo-like about these little enclosures; penguins would not go amiss.

In Oakley's day a stroll through the caverns would emerge at his large, above-ground tropical house, whose French cast-iron pillars (perhaps something the railway magnate Oakley got cheap from a foreign station?) now support the roof of a cattle shed. Harris has taken up the concrete floor to reveal the rockwork and replanted it with a curious mixture of garden and house plants. There is virtually no winter heating at Dewstow, and so any plants suggesting a tropical look must also be pretty hardy. Alongside all this is an extensive rock garden, also replanted.

But it is the caverns themselves that are the magical heart of Dewstow. Narrow paths wind along, lit only by skylights and emerging periodically into chambers of different character. Ferns abound, some familiar from gardens and others from conservatories; both are happily self-sowing on the tufa walls. Spider plants and billbergias share space with vibrantly coloured Solenostemon, Streptocarpus, busy lizzies and fuchsias. One chamber had a ridge roof sticking out above the surface and this now has a temporary roof of polythene to protect its artificial stalactites, ferns and bromeliads.

Water trickles everywhere underground, in pools and waterfalls and fountains. The floors of the tunnels are naturalistically channelled to push aside any escaped water and here and there the path becomes stepping stones. One moment you sidle past craggy, dripping walls, the next you bump into a short run of formal stone balustrade, in the grand Victorian manner (what would Avray Tipping have made of the juxtaposition!). Nothing is sophisticated and yet everything is done with great love and earnest theatricality.

The caverns contain a curious mixture of house plants (Streptocarpus) and hardy plants.

'charmingly
naïve – enjoy it
while you can'

Here and there in the tunnels are little embrasures to hold spirit lamps and in these can be see half-burnt tea lights, evidence of Harris's young family having parties down here. In a few years, no doubt, the garden will become institutionalised, but for now it is the best kind of DIY endeavour and charmingly naïve. Enjoy it while you can: in the south east of England the garden would either be Elton John's private domestic playground, or an earnest, expensive restoration job with hand-held radio guides and a worthy hush in the air.

Left: **Each cavern winds onward to the next.**

Right: **There is something zoo-like about the outdoor enclosures.**

Above: **Some of the original roofs have been lost.**

Dyffryn Fernant

Fishguard, west Wales

'a heart-lifting surprise, a cache of gorgeous, sophisticated gardening at the end of a rough country lane'

Generous cottage gardening swathes the house.

What sets apart a good garden is being alive, developing, having some ambition and polish, working hard at what it does best. There is many a historic garden open to the public which fails miserably on (being alive, developing, having some ambition and polish, working hard at what it does best), which staggers slowly along, its one claim to respect being an ancient and illustrious pedigree; the old whore whose grandfather was an archbishop.

What a blessing it is, then, to find a garden like Dyffryn Fernant, newly maturing and working its socks off. Its ambitions are many: to be colourful at all seasons, to provide a fascinating journey through a score of different spaces and atmospheres, to create some rich and surprising planting. But where it succeeds best, now, is in its relationship to its deep-rural surroundings.

The garden has been made by Christina Shand since she moved here in 1994. It lies in the greenest of flat-bottomed valleys a mile and a half from the sea. To begin with she planted a little enclosed garden in front of the farmhouse and a vegetable garden at the back, and that was the sum of her ambitions. Then gradually she raised her eyes to the challenge of the landscape and now the garden covers 6.5 acres. For her the garden is 'a gut thing', something she has done 'for the place more than for me, a response to it'.

Opposite: **A fine bank of mixed planting leads from the back of the house to the vegetable garden.** Left: **Mercury cocks a leg towards the house's unpretentious galvanised annexe.**

'fine words but what do they mean?'

First, look at the approach to the house. A secluded drive trundles gently downwards along the side of the valley until, suddenly, it has to bend past a rocky outcrop topped by a picturesque ash tree, and there is the house, deep bluish-pink, its barns white-washed or corrugated zinc, and every inch full to bursting with foliage and colour. It is a heart-lifting surprise, a cache of gorgeous, sophisticated gardening at the end of a rough country lane. The little walled front garden is now a collector's fruit cake of pots, seats, paving, so many beloved plants all cuddled together against a house swagged with climbers.

Right: **Meadow appears to run right up to the annexe.**

Opposite: **Looking down to the enclosed front garden from the rough grassy terrace above.**

But now the garden turns you sideways towards the valley floor for its cleverest trick. The valley floor is a water meadow, full of buttercups, meadowsweet, hemp agrimony and billowing grasses of gold, purple and green. Where the garden meets the meadow, a bog garden has been made (gunnera, Joe Pye weed, irises, the usual ornamental suspects) with cruciform paths leading to massive stone seats and, most bravely, a shiny, modern, stainless steel obelisk at its centre. The marvel is that, when the garden and meadow areas are in leaf and flower, there is no telling from the house where one ends and the other begins. A boardwalk then runs across the water meadow through a sea of soft greenery to a pond and a free-flowing stream where flopped willows rise high enough on one elbow to hide completely a colony of young tree ferns (they may or may not survive, but Shand is having a go). Looking back from here, or outwards from the house, the obelisk is a rather wonderful beacon proposing the limit of sophistication and dry land.

This bog-to-meadow arrangement is a response to the valley in practical as well as aesthetic terms, for the land is so rich and moist and the climate so wet that the prairie look, fashionable in the south east of England, would be impossible. Seedheads do not glitter in November frosts here, they collapse in winter rain. The Piet Oudolf school of grasses and perennials has no place here.

Opposite: **Can you see where the bog garden ends and the meadow begins?**

Left: **The pond, out amongst the meadow paths.**

Below: **From meadow to bog garden, the same seamless transition.**

Between the farmhouse, its barns and holiday cottage, there are no big open spaces or lawns. Instead paths weave between colourful shrubs and perennials, sometimes shoulder-high, leading to an endless variety of places to sit. Some are nestled into the rich planting, perhaps of potted lilies and succulents, others are big enough for a table and chairs and a piece of sculpture, others will offer a view out into the valley. The latest stopping place above the house is to be a private grassy hollow where you can lie on your back and see only sky. Nearby, groups of glacial boulders are being exposed to underline the garden's anchorage in the landscape (as do the rock outcrops at Plas Cadnant) and a ruined cottage, probably the original farmhouse, is being excavated to provide another stopping place in the manner of the ruined cottage at The Veddw.

Ferneries set within old walls are a common theme of Welsh gardens (Nant yr Eryd, Plas yn Rhiw), encouraged by the climate and the fact that lime-mortared walls built upon acid soils allow the cultivation of a wider range of species. There is such a garden here too, for exotic ferns, and over its old iron roof members a winter roof of polythene can be thrown. It's where the family takes mulled wine to see in the New Year.

Christina Shand is not a frequent garden visitor, although she still reads voraciously the books of her gurus Christopher Lloyd and Beth Chatto. For her, gardening is about the doing of it more than the observing of it, and her *modus operandi* has been to plant first and refine afterwards, which is a heck of a risk. The bog garden to native water-meadow trick is brilliant; and so

is her sophisticated cottage gardening, bul her desire to plant, and to expand, is getting the better of the garden. There is now a contrived little grass garden, and a symbolic ring of miscellaneous trees. A vast geometric parterre of grasses is elsewhere pushing out into the valley bottom – the antithesis of her bog-to-meadow trick – and gardening is springing up even beyond the pond in the meadow. Shand knows – admits – she has to stop now. If she does, and keeps Dyffryn Fernant so closely tied to its location and its house, it will be a brilliant garden. It's already very, very good.

Oppposite: **House and barns in the verdant landscape.**

Left: **Seats are tucked in everywhere.**

Above: **Sophisticated but easy-going planting.**

Top right: **Grey lamb's lugs, Sambucus 'Black Lace', and a sneaky Ginkgo.**

Right: **Amongst the sophisticated planting are moments that belong entirely to the rustic locale – here just foxgloves and stones.**

Erddig

Wrexham, north Wales

'...is a real breath of fresh air, something one can not often say about a historic garden'

Erddig has old walls aplenty.
Fan trained Plum, 'Early Orleans'.

The house, broken-backed by mining subsidence, and now repaired.

Erddig is a real breath of fresh air, something one can not often say about a historic garden. It has moments of real simplicity as well as its busy moments, and it knows the value of that contrast, and preserves it carefully. It's a lesson every gardener should heed.

Every generation has problems coming to terms with the fashions of the last. We all find our parents' clothes and crockery and bathroom decor unbearably passé. And so it is with gardens. One generation tends to wipe away the fashions of the last, as witness the demise of early eighteenth-century formal gardens at the hands of Capability Brown & Co, who smoothed them away with sinuous lakes and parkland until often no trace of their existence remained.

At Erddig, however, past fashions were tolerated and preserved with an antiquarian patience. Below the east front of the house was an early eighteenth-century garden of formal lawns, closely-trained lime allées, fruit trees and a pond; a restful composition of green structure and geometry; and amazingly, most of it has survived to this day.

Perhaps 'survived' is the wrong word, for by the 1970s the garden was 30ft deep in seedling ash and sycamore trees and the house's back was broken by mining subsidence. Its future looked bleak. Fortunately the National Trust came along, but wanting to take only the furniture. In the end they took the house, the furniture and the garden, giving them all a new lease of life and opening to the public in 1977.

That eastern, formal garden's first escape from destruction came in the 1760s when the landscaper William Eames was called in to undertake remodelling (Eames had a substantial practice in North Wales and the Midlands and also worked at Powis Castle). Eames's work spared the eighteenth-century garden and developed a park, cascade and agricultural improvements on the western side of the house instead. Today Eames's landscape is punctured by a long-defunct slag heap fought over by local government and conservation lobbies; one side wanting to erase an industrial wasteland, the other to preserve our industrial heritage. In fact, if left to cover itself further with trees, this industrial mesa is not a bad addition to the landscape.

In the 1860s Erddig was given another layer of gardening, this time upon the framework of the eighteenth-century garden, but it was discreetly done. To one side, a formal walk was made of pencil yews backed by a running, key-shaped box hedge with filets

of bedding, and backed again by a holly walk. How those Victorians loved their fancy hollies! At the end of the walk was a small formal garden of symmetrical beds set upon shallow terraces. Today the image of that garden has been recreated: Clematis 'Jackmanii' and Rosa 'Dorothy Perkins' rear up like fighting unicorns on tall pyramids, with antirrhinums and patio roses waiting patiently below. Raised quatrefoil beds in Coade stone are home to brightly-coloured bedding. To date, the inevitable exotic Victorian favourites – cannas, cordylines, bananas – have been resisted (see them displayed to perfection at Waddesdon Manor in the Chilterns) and it is wonderful for a change to see this kind of cottage-gardening-on-steroids without architectural foliage. Thank goodness for clarity and restraint. The Victorians did, however, plant their beloved exotic conifers in the park, Wellingtonias and cedars, but the garden proper remained largely uncomplicated by them.

Opposite below: **Victorian yew walk and flower bed of artificial Coade stone.**

Top left and above: **The low-planted Edwardian parterre immediately before the house.**

The Edwardians, too, made their mark on the eighteenth-century garden, setting down a moderately fussy parterre between the house and its low projecting pavilions; a hearth rug to the house's modest fire. It still stands today, but it is tightly planted, hugged close to the house, and interferes little with the serene eighteenth-century prospect.

Very few formal eighteenth-century gardens remain and there is a virtue in saving them for that reason alone. But it is not just their age which makes them so valuable, it is their cool simplicity and, for us today, so used to so much fussy gardening, the contrast they offer. By Victorian standards this is a kind of Minimalism.

This eighteenth-century garden is simple enough. A long gravelled axis runs from the house between rows of potted, topiarised Portugal laurels. Flanking these are clipped yew cones, and apples underplanted with snake's-head fritillaries and narcissi, these in turn backed by a pleached lime allée; and all this leading to a formal pond stocked with mirror carp and backed by tall lime trees, themselves once pleached. Beyond the pond, where once there was a clear opening (clairvoyée) to the landscape beyond, there now stands a formal screen gateway similar to that at Hampton Court Palace or Chirk Castle.

The main vista, flanked by new and ancient lime trees with clipped Portugal laurels.

Daffodils and cherries reflected in the pond.

'there is something clean, contented and gentle
about this large old garden'

Off to one side of all this is an astonishingly long and problematically narrow herbaceous border (250 yards by a meagre 1 yard) with climbers on the wall behind it. It leads to a delightful brick alcove; the whole arrangement is very similar to a long, thin border which ends in the Sulking House at Levens Hall in Cumbria. Keeping any such narrow border constantly interesting is a nightmare, and the one at Erddig does try.

Beyond the pool are other eighteenth-century style features – an allée of scalloped yew hedges for housing bee skeps, another shady alcove – and, rather gracelessly on the walls, grows part of Erddig's National Collection of 100 different ivies. More are grown amongst the service buildings, and in the walled garden, now a car park, is an attractive herb border. There are 180 apple trees.

Like many another large old garden, Erddig is strapped for cash. The pleached limes alone take ten weeks to prune and volunteers are vital to keep the garden going; but still the place manages to shine. There is something clean, contented and gentle about it, something thoroughly alive but never brash. In an age when gardeners are so seduced by full-tilt flower gardening, Erddig is a breath of fresh air.

Erddig's superlative maintenance: pleached lime trees, cones of plain and fastigiate yew, and espalier and fan-trained fruit trees.

Lower House

Hay on Wye, east Wales

'it's not fiddly or sentimental, and although its roots are most definitely in cottage gardening, it has many contemporary elements and attitudes'

Vegetables mark the transition to the wilder parts of the garden.

Lower House is not a name that gives much away. No tale of romance there, no instant temptation. In fact it's an extended stone cottage nestled towards the top of the tiny Dulas valley whose far bank is in England, and it is genuinely romantic; sleepy, with aquamarine paintwork giving a smile of prettiness and its conservatory a firm but unaggressive badge of modernity. The peeling creamy trunks of Asian birches standing in mown grass tell you on arrival that there are gardeners at work here.

Nicky and Peter Daw, whose garden it is, came here in 1985, wanting somewhere with 'easy access to wilderness', in this case the treeless, windswept hilltops above Hay on Wye (Lower House is part of a scattered settlement just outside the town). The garden does not face the wider landscape, it is in a wooded valley, an inward-looking garden, like The Veddw, of small enclosures, streamside and woodland, one moment sunny, another moment dark. It covers 3.5 acres and there is the same amount again of grazing land on which the Daws keep a few sheep, neither wilderness nor garden. The winds may blow up top, but down here it is absolutely silent except for the sound of water.

Low-key paintwork and a plain wood conservatory disturb neither the countryside nor the sheep.

'clipped box bubbles form duckling queues'

It is a hard-working plantsman's garden around the house, but towards the edges it becomes progressively lower key; the banks of the stream are kept wild, and rough grass filled with cowslips and fritillaries makes a quiet transition to their pasture land above. The Daws absolutely hate Lower House being called a cottage garden (so they do at The Veddw) and rightly so; it's not fiddly or sentimental, and although its roots are most definitely in cottage gardening, it has many contemporary elements and attitudes.

The beginning is genial and bucolic. Like many an old agricultural cottage, its drive comes to the side of the house, leaving you slightly unsure where to start. There are sheds a few steps short of tumbledown, which form the backdrop for what was once a potager and is now a cuddlesome planting of herbs and grasses. Clipped box bobbles of various sizes form duckling queues here and there, defining the layout, and one or two are being cloud-pruned.

Cypresses show their age in the old potager.

Grasses and topiary forms give substance to the old potager.

But this isn't the real way in. For that you must sneak through a porch and a tree fern alley to find the front of the house which is seriously, lazily, stylishly pretty. (This is the way the Daws bring in their B&B guests, for the big surprise). Here a secluded semi-circle of lawn pushes down to the shady streamside, table and chairs sit under a tree, and against the house blue Clematis 'Perle d'Azur' meanders high into the branches of a silver-variegated Rhamnus alaternus. The enormous magnolia dates from long before the Daws' time, and cypresses, starting to show their flabby middle-age, rise up behind it.

'B&B, all ye who enter here!'
Clematis 'Polish Spirit' (left) and
'Perle d'Azur' (right).

The temptation now is to head for the wood-and-stone conservatory, open both sides like a monumental gateway; inside it's a glorious tumble-dryer of climbers and pot plants. Pass through it and there is the core of the entire garden, a small, gravelled yard, sunk into the hill on two sides, and bounded by the house and conservatory on the others. Much of the yard – too much for my comfort – is taken up by a shallow ziggurat of paving, in effect a triple crossing of two stone stairways and a pair of spouting water tanks. It's a curious construction, slightly clumsy to my eye, an unsettled focus, but beautifully welded into position by spreading pools of acaena that sometimes even spread across a whole path. Local stone is used throughout, except for the lower tank which is made of sawn slate and strikes a distracting note of chic. The architectural theme continues into the planting, made with the exotic foliage of bananas, cannas and a huge Tetrapanax wrapped every winter to get it through the cold. It's all very luscious and excellently grown, and never too studied.

House garden and wild garden meet at a gap in the wall.

The sophisticated ziggurat of stairs, devoted more to getting out of the little courtyard than to being in it. A medlar grows in its brick circle.

Above: **Acaena 'Kupferteppich' flows across the paving.**

Thereafter the less sophisticated gardening begins. There is a kitchen garden surrounded by hornbeam hedges, and a rustic rond-point, of mown paths cut through longer meadow grass, is centred on a small stone dolmen. Then it's off into the wood, the 'wild garden'.

The woodland walk is just a single-width trodden path, a thinking path, that winds its way quietly across the brook and up amongst trunks of beech and mature Douglas firs, where bluebells, snowdrops and ferns cover the slope below. Crossing back, a small wild pond has been made, nestled amongst the great leaves of gunnera and a billowing bank of the yellow leaved dogwood, Cornus alba 'Aurea'. Peter Daw was told the garden showed 'a light touch' on its surroundings and he's proud of it. (The revetments, built to control the Dulas brook which periodically tries to change its course through the wood, are almost invisible but vital; several bridges have been washed away).

Left: **Grey Kniphofia caulescens and red Crocosmia 'Lucifer' in the exotic bed.**

Above: **Verbena bonariensis.**

Right: **A cairn in the woodland garden.**

Left: **The fat trunk and huge leaves of Tetrapanax papyrifer.**

Opposite: **Boundary trees in the woodland garden.**

But will the touch stay so light? In all gardens there is a tendency always to become that little bit more polished, that little bit more sophisticated, less rough, less simple. Yes, the old cypresses are getting shabby and must go; the Daws know it. Yes, maybe the time has come for the picturesque old sheds and decrepit outhouse walls to be renovated and given a new use; they will only collapse given no attention at all. But what of cloud-pruning yet more box bushes, of the fancy ferns planted in the wood, the delightful new bamboo grove, the inscribed slate stele politely proposing wilderness? If the centre of the garden becomes ever more smart – that slate tank – then can the edges of the garden remain so unimproved next to the wilderness? Low-key gardening is so difficult to do; it is so hard to resist adding that one extra detail, the tipping point, until suddenly that restful, desired, undeveloped ordinariness is gone. The road to chic is paved with good intentions.

Nant-yr-Eryd

Pembrokeshire, west Wales

'it's bizarre, fascinating, and delightfully, ruthlessly masculine'

The red paintwork is beguiling and exclusive at the same time.

Say cottage gardening and people come over all Rosemary Verey, itsy-bitsy pinks and low thatched eaves. Cosy Edwardian stuff. But cottage gardening does not have to be that way. Sometimes it can be cool and plain and shine for its simplicity alone, and such a garden is Nant-yr-Eryd, perhaps because its creator is a man, Alan Hall, a professional landscaper. There is nothing remotely feminine about Nant-yr-Eryd. Hall's wife Diana is allowed to put her spoke in occasionally, but that's all.

Hall is a third-generation nurseryman. His father worked for the famous Russell's nursery and as a boy he would tag along with his father on landscaping jobs. In 1981 he built a garden at Chelsea Show. Today he works as a freelance landscape gardener for three to four mornings a week. He and his wife upped sticks from Hampshire in the late 1970s to take on this little house and farmsteading where, until they came, 1000 pigs were reared. They knew the area from having taken walking holidays here years ago. Once the house was made good, Hall started on his garden, bringing back several mature topiary pieces from his Chelsea garden to get it off to a good start.

Proof of the garden's no-nonsense masculinity is the house itself. A concrete path runs along the front of it, slap bang against the wall. There is none of that romantic profusion of climbers to be seen at Dyffryn Fernant or Lower House. Here everything is resolutely plain, the only concession to colour being the red paint around the doors and windows. Even the unpainted seals that flank the front door stand symmetrically. There used to be little beds against the house wall, but Hall emptied them and concreted them over. No nonsense at all.

A simple house with its patch of rough meadow garden.

Out in the open part of the garden is a similarly robust feature, a plank bench on stone legs set within a clipped semicircle of the bush honeysuckle, Lonicera nitida. Behind this, and in fact throughout the garden, are simple country plants such as evening primrose, mulleins, crambe and the pale pink hardy Fuchsia magellanica var 'Molinae'. The bench sits looking out towards the landscape beyond the garden, a scene of traditional, pastoral agriculture; and yet for much of the year the view is hidden by a border of roses and perennials just inside the fence. The roses are Hall's gift to Mrs Hall, and the adjacent border is the garden's flowery heart, planted with 'William Lobb', 'Bonica', Rosa mundi, 'Souvenir de la Malmaison' and 'Albertine'. "I am a daffodil man, myself," explains Hall, which is why, to demonstrate their favourite kinds of plant, the garden opens for the National Gardens Scheme in March and June.

Roses, lilies, sweet williams, and topiary armchairs, the essence of cottage gardening.

There are areas of long grass which, if not exactly a romantic wildflower meadow, he has filled with bulbs, cultivated forms of meadow cranesbills and ox-eye daisies to beef up the effect, and between the old sheds and a stacked-slate garden wall there are banks of hardy pink geraniums.

A further masculine touch is a blocked window embrasure, framed in carved wood and shelved from side to side to make an auricula theatre. But Hall chooses not to trouble himself with the niceties of growing auriculas and decorates this cabinet of curiosities with busy lizzies or whichever plant of the season looks smart.

Like so many small Welsh gardens, Hall has incorporated many of the old farm buildings into the garden. In this case he has gardened the ruined pig houses. There have been almost no repairs made, and it is all a million miles from the Ninfarium at Aberglasney which houses tender rarities. Nor is this any kind of idealised ruin in the manner of the sham castles at Bodysgallen or Plas Brondanw. Here are just crumbling old stone sheds; inside, chunks of mortar hang out from the walls, black, decayed rafters span the upper storey, ivy slithers where it will, and farmerly concrete plays its inevitable role at ground level.

Geranium x oxonianum spreads across a rough lawn.

Left: **Hypericum calycinum feels free to colonise an old wall.**

Above: **Begonias in the bookshelf theatre.**

There are native ferns, in their plain and frilly forms, and slightly tender exotic species (Woodwardia radicans, Dicksonia antarctica) which thrive because a polythene sheet can be slung over the rafters in winter, just as at Dyffryn Fernant.

The individual pig pens have been blocked up to form lily tanks and gunnera becomes truly dramatic in such a confined space. But still there is an unstudied air of abandonment to the sheds: young thorn and ash trees arch over the planting and a

droopy Mexican pine, Pinus patula, promises to provide a roof in future years. In the next roofless shed, several farrowing pens and steel crates have been planted to support rampant rambling roses, a task for which they will surely be inadequate.

Opposite: **Ferns in the old piggeries.**

Above: **Lily tanks and giant Gunnera.**

Topiary garden by the house.

Tucked beside the house is an extraordinary topiary garden, of yew and box shapes set within lightly castellated hedges of Leyland cypress. No flower beds in amongst the topiary pieces (although there is a spring carpet of snowdrops beneath), just a cheerful, irregular chess board of jostling, abstract shapes; pigs in a pen, you might say. What lifts the picture artistically as well as visually is the development of three floating thorn bobbles created along the top of the tall thorn hedge behind. At this moment, garden meets country in a delightful green compromise (although the gardener is of course the outright winner).

Through the hedge on the edge of an open field is Hall's latest piece of garden. Wire stock fencing surrounds a convocation of young topiary pieces, set out in a more or less symmetrical fashion. The soil between them is bare but immaculately hoed. It is a school for topiary pieces, fenced in to stop them running off like piglets. It's bizarre, fascinating, and delightfully, ruthlessly masculine, just like the rest of the garden.

Above left : **Thorn bobbles tease the topiary out into the countryside.**

Above right: **The most recent area of topiary – cast out of the garden?**

National Botanic Garden of Wales

Carmarthen, south west Wales

'it is already becoming an enduring icon for Wales'

Red astilbes, pink astrantia and yellow ligularia in the bog garden.

After massive investment from the Millennium Commission, Lottery and Welsh Assembly, the National Botanic Garden of Wales opened in 2000. Such is the political climate today, that money can be found for capital works, for buildings and roads and infrastructure, but when it comes to ongoing running costs – jobs and people – funds are much harder to find. It is unfortunate for gardens, because continuity of care is their life blood. A garden meant for education and science has even greater needs.

The NBGW was the only wholly new botanic garden to open in the 20th century and expected by its masters to break even on costs in only a few years, whereas Kew had begun life as a well-endowed royal palace, has had 200 years to become a by-word for horticulture, and continues to receive massive funding. The poor NBGW was starting completely from scratch and had a hugely tough start; like a heavily-loaded plane trying to get off the ground with too little fuel. Now at last the plane is in the air, extraordinarily beautiful in parts, wobbly in others, but truly deserving of everybody's goodwill. Wales has a botanic garden at last.

The Great Glasshouse rises above luscious perennials and, right, the beginnings of a summer meadow garden.

**The Great Glasshouse by Sir Norman Foster,
part hill, part spaceship.**

The garden's £9 million Great Glasshouse has to be one of the most beautiful modern buildings in Britain, an elliptical dome emerging flawless amongst other green hills. Money well spent. It is already becoming an enduring icon for Wales, as Kew's Palm House is for London and the biomes of the Eden Project are for Cornwall.

Designed by Sir Norman Foster, one of our great contemporary architects, it set a standard for impressively well-made buildings and hard landscaping throughout the garden (how unadventurous by comparison is the Royal Horticultural Society's new glasshouse at Wisley, built to commemorate its bicentenary).

Two further strong, modern buildings help to anchor the garden to the landscape: first a tropical house full of steamy ferns, gingers and orchids, designed by the New York architect John Belle; second, a suite of education buildings, as cool and stylish as any New England weekend retreat, which perches out over one of the garden's several lakes (the eighteenth-century landscape park of Middleton House underlies the garden, and it is heavily pushed as the part of the garden's credentials).

Left: **Schools buildings over one of the ponds.**

Above: **Tropical House by New York architect John Belle.**

Events and education form a major part of the garden's programme.

Like any botanic garden today, a major part of its remit is education and there are permanent facilities for school use as well as a 360 degree cinema to make you unexpectedly intimate with the world's flora. There are programmes for adult learning too, courses where people can learn about specialist areas of horticulture such as ferns, fungi, orchids, pharmacy and, of course, practical gardening. Sensibly too, in this age of the digital camera, there are courses in photography.

Within the double-walled garden (one walled enclosure within another) are beds demonstrating ornamentally the different families of plants and showing what odd bedfellows they contain. The initial planting was far too thick and close, possibly misleading the domestic gardener; but still everything is well-maintained and cared for. Outside the walled garden is the Broadwalk, a long, flamboyant flower border and rill, along which visitors walk as they enter the garden. It lacks a designed end or a beginning, rather it just starts then stops; but, as they say, it's the journey that counts. Nearby, on the edge of the lakes, a zigzag board walk disappears into a particularly successful bog garden.

Developing borders in the double walled garden.

These are features you might not be surprised to see in a botanic garden, but the NBGW does more. The hill on which the Great Glasshouse stands is a meadow garden, richly spangled not with wildflowers but paeonies, irises, Lychnis coronarius and many more species. In July it is an extraordinary sight, and all for the price of one cut per year from a heavy-duty mower. The climate may deny the NBGW a winter forest of tall seedheads turning silver in the frost, (there is the same problem at Dyffryn Fernant), but still it is a remarkable sight.

Across the lake is the 20 acre 'Woods of the World', where tree species from the different continents are being planted on a grand scale. Where else might you see 100 young monkey puzzles rearing their spiky heads? Beyond this the NBGW owns a large area of species-rich farmland now designated a National Nature Reserve. It is an extraordinary resource.

And inside that Great Glasshouse? It is truly thrilling to enter that main door and see its unsupported 60m steel arches, stretched one after another against the sky. It seems so much bigger on the inside and, since the land inside is deeply excavated, far taller too. The renowned American landscape designer, Kathryn Gustafson, designed its rolling, naturalistic interior landscape, and it is planted with a flora from the six Mediterranean climates of the world, Chile, South Africa, Australia, California and the Mediterranean basin, whose rich but threatened flora has 2% of the earth's surface and 20% of its species.

The Mediterranean climate is hot and dry in summer and cool and moist in winter, giving the glasshouse an extraordinary flowering of trees, shrubs, bulbs and perennials in spring. A gorge runs down the centre of Gustafson's design, ending in a rather stark basement space with cloudy pool and waterfalls. It's meant to be the antidote to the baking summer landscape, and it is, but for me it also has an air of abandoned foundations for a skyscraper. Time may show it to be an emperor in new clothing.

Some said the NBGW was made too far from centres of population (Cardiff, 55 mins; Swansea, 30 mins.) It's far enough, perhaps, but the position has huge advantages which can only become rarer and more important with every passing year: clean air, a romantic topography upon which to make an exciting garden, a landscape and ecology which invite a promising cooperation, not exclusion. One day soon the value (and the bravery) of this location will be appreciated; Kew itself, remember, was in the country when it was first begun. Support it.
Stick by it.

The interior of the Great Glasshouse, designed by Kathryn Gustafson, displays plants from those sections of the world with a Mediterranean climate. With a sunken floor and a high arching roof, the sense of space is enormous.

Bottom row left to right:

Helianthus annuus 'Ring of fire'

Galtonia viridiflora, with Yucca gloriosa 'Variegata' in foreground.

Dryandra formosa

Helenium 'Waldtraut'

Protea cynaroides

Top row left to right:

Santolina rosmarinifolia, Helenium 'Pumilum Magnificum', and purple phormium.

Cyrtanthus falcatus

Xanthorrhoea

Scilla peruviana

Phylica pubescens

Plas Brondanw

Llanfrothen, north Wales

'it's a real place with a genuine atmosphere.
And like Portmeirion it's fun, only more seriously so'

Heroic sculpture abounds.

Like Harlech Castle, Portmeirion village is one of the icons of the west coast of Wales, and it's great fun. It was constructed by the architect Sir Clough Williams-Ellis between 1925-1973, a faux Italian village of brightly-coloured stucco, trompe l'oeil painting and scraps of architectural salvage that Clough Williams-Ellis (let's call him CWE) could not bear to see lost. It's a glorious salvage yard, a stage set (they filmed *The Prisoner* for television here), now holiday cottages, tourist shops and a hotel; it's an architectural capriccio like the great Whistler mural at Plas Newydd.

But it's barely a garden. It has gardening, true, but it's not a garden. CWE's real garden is at his home Plas Brondanw up the road and it's one of the best gardens in Wales. It's a real place with a genuine atmosphere. And like Portmeirion it's fun, only more seriously so.

'a classical
garden of vistas,
viewpoints and
perspectives

The garage and boy fireman at the entrance to the garden.

Plas Brondanw itself is now let and made into flats and so, as often happens in these circumstances, visitors to the garden must arrive in the least appealing place – the garages. What you immediately see is an oddly-placed little pool with a statuette of a boy fireman holding his piddling hose. It's a joke and (though you'd never know it yet) a reference to the house fire in 1951. It seems so tacky. So let's forget him and start again, as if we were coming out of the house with CWE. We will descend through the tall bulwark tower that he built to prop up the old 1660 house and come out halfway along his great yew-hedged vista with the mountain shining at one end. That's better.

Now this is not going to be a flower garden, although it is not short of flowers. Rather it's a classical garden of vistas and viewpoints and perspectives, taking every advantage of the surrounding dramatic landscape. Everything is defined and punctuated by dark yew hedges, topiary, gates, balustrades and the occasional piece of sculpture, of CWE's heroes like the architect Inigo Jones and even the firemen who saved his house. There is the formality and flavour of a Chiswick House, but all on a modest scale, domestic though far from miniature like Iford Manor. It is a magnificently liveable garden.

The main transverse vista under the house, lined with Japanese anemones.

Topiary and yew hedges are what make
Plas Brondanw such fun.

The land slopes downwards from the house and so inevitably there is terracing and balustrades (CWE's ubiquitous ornate ironwork is painted a joyful turquoise and yellow, signature colours he also used at Portmeirion and meant to be a poor man's verdigris and gold).

Classical sculpture and the signature of gold-and-verdigris paintwork add a touch of pomp.

Below that yew-hedged vista is a wide sloping lawn, at the centre of which is an odd but very satisfying feature that only CWE would have come up with: here, at the junction with yet another vista, is a massive evergreen oak – dark, strong, faintly scruffy, a man's tree if ever there was – and under its shady canopy CWE erected an oval platform within heavy balustrading to create a sense of stillness and calm, a galleon in a sea of lawn.

Equally weighty is CWE's classical orangery which stands at the centre of the garden, at a transition from the oak lawn to a matrix of smaller, more enclosed spaces. There are loud echoes here of the orangery at Hestercombe, built by Lutyens in 1904 and which also marks a transition from one part of a garden to another.

Past the orangery is a grid of lightly-planted, geometric, sculpture-bearing enclosures where hedged allées criss-cross and, from a raised platform at the far end, you can see all the way back to the piddling pompier and his hose pipe; as a comic focus he makes sense at last.

You might think you had seen all the garden now, but not so; CWE had much bigger plans. Cross the road, go through the fine blue and gold gates, and you are in a landscape garden, where a glimpse of one Picturesque feature leads you upward to the next until you reach the castle at the top of the hill. Right now it is sad and overgrown in equal measure, but you must see it.

Far left: **The evergreen oak platform and view to the mountains.**

Lower left: **The orangery.**

Above left: **Centurion seen through pleached limes.**

Above: **Verdigris paint links even the built features.**

From those first gates, a narrow avenue connects (though you would never know it) the house and a monumental urn raised in 1953 in memory of the great fire. From here you can look way down into a (once) formal pool and cascade. Behind you, what looks like a striped Henry V bus shelter lost under the trees is a painted gazebo from which to admire another dramatic (and lost) vista. Walk on up the hill and you come to CWE's hilltop castle, funded as a wedding present by his fellow Guards officers (it beats silver plate). It's only 25ft high but from below it looks vast, and when you climb up inside you can see for ever.

Or at least you should be able to, but even here on the hilltop trees are gradually becoming the undoing of Plas Brondanw. Yes, they are lovely, dark and deep, but they are ruining every carefully contrived view, even from within the formal garden; the great Welsh pioneers of the Picturesque movement must be tearing out their hair, and quite right. Like Hafod, Plas Brondanw needs the chainsaws, scrupulously managed, to let it breathe, and what stands in the way is not just insufficient funding but inappropriate woodland management. What matters here – one of Wales most important gardens of any period, or trees which in this part of the world are weeds? It is shameful that this formal garden just about survives and the landscape garden sits and rots.

From the bottom of the garden back to the boy fireman.

Plas Brondanw must have help and restoration. Not by larding it up with easy flowers to pull in the Portmeirion punters – let Powis and Bodnant have all the real flowery fireworks, they do it so well – but by making Plas Brondanw what underneath it still is, a clever, cool, joyful and rare garden.

Left: **Abandoned cascade and pool.**

Above: **The Outlook Tower, a sham castle, was a gift to CWE and his wife from his fellow Welsh Guards.**

Plas Cadnant

Anglesey, north Wales

'a small piece of Hafod on Anglesey;
a lily that requires no gilding, only sunlight
and a little clearance'

Welsh bluebells in the woodland garden.

Plas Cadnant is a 'gentrified farm' as its present owner Anthony Tavernor calls it, big but not grand. Tavernor is a farmer, and farmers tend to fall into two kinds, the rigorously organised kind, and the make-do-and-mend, get-there-in-the-end kind. Tavernor is definitely one of the former, and having taken on Plas Cadnant he is quietly doing a Heligan without all the fuss and funding. Or doing a Dewstow, where farmer John Harris is restoring his garden of twentieth century grottoes.

Farming in Staffordshire, Tavernor bought Plas Cadnant in 1996 as a small agricultural investment. The house was built in 1803 by John Price, agent to the Marquis of Anglesey at Plas Newydd five miles away. Plas Cadnant's heyday was 1918-1939, was let in the 1940s, and in decline ever since. By 1996 it was a mess; the service buildings were crumbling and the walled garden was effectively woodland; Tavernor had no idea Plas Cadnant had a garden. Luckily he had always been a passionate visitor to houses and gardens and the place turned out to be all his hobbies rolled into one. It is now very much his home.

Tavernor has a matter-of-fact attitude to repair and regeneration; not for him the kind of slavish devotion to history which prefers nothing to be done if there is no precise record of what was there originally. (At Wales's greatest Picturesque landscape, Hafod near Aberystwyth, 100 men with 100 chain saws could begin to show what that landscape had to say in a month, yet the landscape remains covered in a meaningless smothering of ill-placed forestry, while conservationists and the authorities appear to fight over architectural details. It is heartbreaking.)

Now Plas Cadnant is a trifle compared to Hafod, but still it is a pretty garden and it deserves consideration and loving care, which is what it gets from Tavernor. From being new in the world of gardens, everybody now seems to know him; he puts himself about, he talks to people, he reads, he researches, he takes all the advice he can get. Then he gets on and does something personal and bold.

Taking on a project like this can be daunting and even depressing, so Tavernor has allowed himself a treat every year, to see something finished and looking good. After

fixing the house therefore (the service buildings are now holiday cottages) he turned one of the yards behind the house into a box-edged herb garden but then rightly held his nerve and kept the large farmyard perfectly plain except for some perimeter borders.

Below the house is the walled garden, nestled in a wide gully. Unfortunately the land slopes in two directions at once and, in such a situation, levels and lines always seem uncomfortable with each other. The original design handled the problem perfectly by making the bottom wall dip

down in what is called a catenary curve, of the kind a rope makes when stretched between two poles. It is both elegant and relaxed. Nature's compromise.

The house and walled garden, showing the developing yew pyramids and, at the bottom end, the pond and beautifully curved wall.

Intent on some serious flower gardening rather than two acres of vegetables, Tavernor scooped up great volumes of soil to create a raised walk down one side of the garden, flanked by vast parallel herbaceous borders. They run from blues and yellows at the top to reds at the bottom and are planted for late colour, to follow on from spring woodland gardening elsewhere. The bedroom of the holiday cottage looking straight down these borders must have one of the most privileged views anywhere, unless you prefer lagoon hotels, palms and infinity pools.

Long, bold borders look across to a triangle of older planting.

Top: **The cottage garden.**

Left: **The herb garden.**

Middle: **Clipped holly and box slabs.**

The upper sections of the long borders
with developing topiary accents.

In the main bowl of the walled garden Tavernor is making a simple cross of marching yew and hornbeam cones which, one day, may be big enough to command the space if he let's them get so big. If not, it will always look rather empty. Opposite his new borders will be an answering 70 yard border of bold foliage, punctuated by a new pavilion, the design of which is exercising him mightily. At the top of the garden he is growing old Welsh varieties of fruit such as the pear 'Snowdon Queen' and the 'Bardsey' and 'Pig's Snout' apples. At the bottom he has unusually lost his nerve and retained a muddly triangle of old lady's shrubbery gardening which might be better started again.

Below: **The walled garden and pool from bottom to top. How uncomfortable a pool can look on rising ground.**

Opposite clockwise from top left: **Achillea, Echinacea 'Ruby Giant', Angelica gigas, Evergreen azalea 'White Lady', Rhododendron 'Winsome', and Pieris formosa var. forrestii 'Wakehurst'.**

Garden historian Sir Roy Strong likes to provoke his audiences by saying that 'a gardener who resorts to plants has failed'. And indeed the risk to Plas Cadnant is that Tavernor is becoming a collector-plantsman. The woodland garden he has thinned drastically and quite right too, and now he is filling it with a breathtaking array of flowering trees and shrubs and woodland and waterside perennials which, in their season, will be striking indeed. Azaleas, rhododendrons, maples, eucryphias, they are all here; hellebores, gunnera, primulas, astilbes, meconopsis, the works.

But where to stop? The parkland has a number of wooded, Picturesque rock hillocks, the largest of which was already gardened, and this too is back on the road to a full underplanting of ornamentals.

Primulas and bluebells in the woodland garden.

Left: **Wooded outcrops characterise the park.**

Opposite: **The perfect little Picturesque gorge, approached by its 39 steps.**

Yet still – where to stop? Beyond the woodland garden is a truly Picturesque little valley where a small river drops between mossy, quartz-streaked cliffs and rock pools, offering secluded romantic viewpoints. A small piece of Hafod on Anglesey; a lily that requires no gilding, only sunlight and a little clearance. Tavernor the Brave is in there finding old paths, making new ones, felling gangly sycamores and 30ft laurels and invasions of rhododendron scrub. He's a marvel of energy. But will he have the nerve, or is it the discipline, to stop planting here and keep it green, or perhaps stick to just a couple of ornamental species planted *en masse* as if they lived here naturally? No doubt the valley dell at Bodnant had its Picturesque attractions before it was filled with exotic shrubs and conifers and turned into a 'garden'; today everyone loves the dell, it's amazing, but we cannot know if we would prefer it without the exotics. At Plas Cadnant there is still time to preserve and keep distinct this little gem of the Picturesque, something Wales was so good at.

Plas Newydd

Anglesey, north Wales

'each piece of this garden is an island unto itself'

Azaleas in the woodland garden.

It is something about the reflected light and its waterside position that makes Plas Newydd so fresh. There it sits on the shore of the Menai Straits, to the left George Stephenson's Britannia Bridge, and in front across the water the wooded shore of the mainland with the mountains of Snowdonia rising behind. There is always something special about looking out over water to land again: a view of open sea is empty, implying unfathomable distances, but a strait, or a great river like the Rhine or the Grand Canal in Venice, implies traffic, shipping, trade, activity. Life.

In the days before bridges, when Anglesey was truly an island, a waterside position made every sense. But approaching a grand house from the land, when it stands on the shore at the bottom of a steep slope, is inevitably less than elegant. By the 1790s Plas Newydd had a comfortable fortune in coal and copper, and its environs were remodelled by the landscape designer Humphrey Repton, the work including an approach that slid around behind the house to arrive obliquely down the slope towards the house and water, to lessen the gradient. If only there were some better way for the visiting public to approach today than down a steep and inappropriately civic outdoor staircase (when you get to the bottom, shake your head, forget about it, and start again).

Across the Menai Straits to the mainland and Snowdonia.

In the late 19th century the 5th Marquis of Anglesey built a conservatory onto the back of the house to the north, but his penchant for the theatre, frocks and jewellery frittered away much of the family fortune. During the 1920-1930s his cousin the 6th Marquis put the family house in order, knocking down his cousin's conservatory and replacing it with a series of Italian terrace gardens: a miniature Bodnant, one might say, but still rather semi-detached and tucked away at the back, if more sheltered for that. South of the house he planted conifers to keep out the wind. Indoors, he made the house unusually comfortable for its day ('every bathroom must have a bedroom') and created a new dining room, for which he commissioned the grandest of Rex Whistler's *trompe l'oeil* murals – appropriately enough, a waterside architectural capriccio.

Above: **North up the Straits to George Stephenson's Britannia Bridge.**

Left and opposite: **Terracotta jars, statuary, waterworks and treillage on the terraces.**

When the present 7th Lord Anglesey succeeded to the title in 1947, aged 25, the place was shabby and in difficulties, but he picked up the baton and revived it. He married, brought up a family, and in 1976 gave Plas Newydd to the National Trust, whose principal interest was a room with a view (by Whistler, and of Snowdonia). It was one of the last houses and gardens to be taken by the Trust without a financial endowment for its upkeep.

With the future secure, the Marquis and the National Trust, began to develop the garden as seen today. Year by year the 1920s terraces were enriched, creating an echo in creeper-clad treillage of the old conservatory around a tufa grotto, and making long colourful borders, superbly planted and maintained, and a series of formal pools descending through the various terraces (it is time to stop now; the most recent feature, which has escaped beyond the terraces, is an insubstantial rill under the shade of conifers).

The terrace hot borders, with marigolds, Sedum, Dahlia 'David Howard', Ricinius 'Carmencita', Helenium, Canna, Crocosmia, Rudbeckia, Miscanthus, and Argyranthemum.

South of the house a woodland garden was begun amongst the old cypresses planted by the Marquis's father. Grassy sweeps and glades are fringed with maples, and cherries, and jolly mounds of loud hydrangeas sit like pastel meringues in the grass. Cleverly, windows have been cut in the shoreline shelter trees at high and low level, offering views of both the mountains and the water, but without losing wind protection. Occasionally honey fungus will kill a mature tree, but that's life in a woodland garden; a gardener has to be resigned to it.

The 'West Indies' with great clumps of hydrangeas.

'the trees have been thinned irregularly,
by man and by time'

Above: **Pollard oak.**

Right: **Pollard limes with wild garlic.**

The last part of the garden to be developed was a new arboretum of Australasian trees, replacing a worn-out orchard. It sounds dreary and it is anything but. Many species of eucalyptus and later southern beeches (Nothofagus) were planted in groups but on a grid, like an orchard. It had every promise of being boring, but actually time has worked wonders. The trees have been thinned irregularly, by man and by time, to produce a meandering woodland where everything seems greeny-grey. Some species are naturally erect, others naturally slight or scrubby, producing a natural, ungardened effect. In the glades, leathery phormiums stand bizarrely amongst carpets of native orchids. At one point a number of Eucalyptus dalrympleana have been left in grid to form the pillars of a 'green cathedral', with grey-green walls of pittosporum. If you were asked to locate a picture of this arboretum, the last place on earth you would expect it to be is Wales. It is an extraordinary flash of novelty, produced as much by management as initial design, but still it is a delight and, in its way, the perfect complement to the open grey skies and reflecting waters around the house.

Pollard oak above a bank of white Azalea 'Palestrina'.

Eucalyptusw oodland.

Top right: **The rhododendron garden.**

What a contrast, then, to march ¾ mile north to the rhododendron garden, a few acres of massive old Scots pines under which is planted a fine collection of rhododendrons of all kinds: large, small, early, late, hybrid and species. Lorry loads of them came as presents from Bodnant. It is only open during the flowering season, so it hardly forms part of the average visit, but at the right time it's a gem.

There is a freshness and unexpectedness about all of Plas Newydd. The house, when you reach it, has its back to you, eyes on the water. But then, like a sitting hen, it will flap one wing and there to one side is an arboretum; flap the other and there, with all too little relation to the house, are the terraces. Flap a bit harder and you get a rhododendron garden. Each piece of this garden is an island unto itself.

Plas yn Rhiw

Pwllheli, north Wales

'it feels personal, warm and genial; everyone can see themselves living here and loving it'

Water pours out amongst liverworts and ferns.

What use is good design and good planting if it does not bring an individual atmosphere to a garden? At Plas yn Rhiw on the Llŷn Peninsula, the design and the planting are charmingly lackadaisical, mudded even, but they combine to make an extraordinary atmosphere. It feels personal, warm and genial; everyone can see themselves living here and loving it.

Plas yn Rhiw is what one would call a period piece, although which period is open to discussion. The house itself is a seventeenth-century farmhouse overlooking Hell's Mouth Bay; but given a very pretty make-over in Regency times, including a verandah running the whole length of the house. Sanctified in the 1920s by the architect Clough Williams-Ellis (see Plas Brondanw) as a gem of vernacular Welsh architecture, it fell into serious disrepair until in 1939 it was bought by three spinster friends of Williams-Ellis, the sisters Eileen, Lorna and Honora Keating. They found it a wonderful jungle of vast bay trees, fuchsias and figs, and so many brambles guarded the door that the sisters could only view the property by sneaking in through a window.

The sisters made extensive repairs to the house and went on to open it to the public. Parts of the interior walls were stripped of their plaster to show the old stonework beneath, in the same way that people today strip off Victorian paintwork to show 'real' wood. In 1952 the sisters gave Plas yn Rhiw to the National Trust which took over its direct care in 1981 when Lorna, the last sister, died.

Above: **The parterre and Hell's Mouth Bay.**

Today the Trust reckons to show the house as it was when she died, but in fact it has undergone a great deal of tidying up since then; it appears far more 1950s than 1980s, yet still the atmosphere is beguiling: the fur coats on the back of the doors, Honora's watercolours on the stairs, the pots and pans, the 'modern' television.

Above: **Rustic stone seats.**

Right: **The semi-circular top terrace.**

And what of the garden the sisters loved so well? Spread before the verandah is a plain semicircular lawn, enclosed and protected from the drop beyond by a fat box hedge above which there is a wonderful view of the sky and the bay. Make the most of this view for, apart from a perfect little viewpoint bench just below the hedge, it is the only significant view the garden offers. Thereafter it's all nuzzling amongst the bushes. Here is the age-old problem of exposed gardens (compare Wyndcliffe Court): do you have views and wild winds, or shelter and no view?

On a slope below this terrace is a late nineteenth-century, cottagey parterre of box hedges interplanted with a colourful mixture of shrubs and perennials. Everything is mixed at Plas yn Rhiw, there is nothing strict, nothing studied. Even the pattern of formal beds is very far from symmetrical and the hedges themselves are thigh-high and chunky, not stringy little patterns around one's ankles. To reinforce this easy-going atmosphere, the parterre is invisible from the upper lawn and overlooked only by the upper floors of the house – a parent keeping just half an eye on its charge, a ruffian garden sent out to play.

The parterre from below, with Clematis montana.

Beyond the parterre, the garden becomes a series of garden rooms and winding paths, separated by unexpected little gates and chicanes of clipped yew. Now it would be unfair to call Plas yn Rhiw shabby and it's certainly not shabby chic, but it does have an admirably low-key maintenance style. Like most gardens (not least those belonging to the National Trust) it is understaffed, having just one gardener and a few volunteers, but the result here is hugely appealing.

There is a feeling of work to be done, of an owner, not a horde of gardeners, about to come out and potter and fix things personally. There are no labels and signs. The narrow entrances and exits speak of one person at a time; the grass paths worn bare down the centre by passing feet (only 14,000 pairs a year) show a gently tolerated domestic problem. What a disaster for the atmosphere it would be to bring in lorry loads of squeaky-clean, institutional gravel or bark.

Nature's green glove.

Hedges, ferns and flowers are the
mainstay of the garden.

Gates and gateways are an important feature; centre, flanked by Euphorbia mellifera.

When it came to planting the three sisters did not agonise about where things should go: they were plonkers, not placers. In their early days they wrote to the Trust asking for smaller gardens to be given plants from the larger gardens, and this may account for the presence of some most uncottagey species – a great tree of the rare Berberis valdiviana, odd South African watsonias sitting like leathery gladioli amongst the camellias. The largest magnolias are now the size of forest trees. Many of the old roofless outbuildings are incorporated into the garden but only very lightly planted, perhaps with a ground-row of ferns or a swag of wisteria or a clump of Japanese anemone growing out of a wall.

Behind the house is a grassy glade for picnicking. One could begin to tart it up (someone has) with fancy little trees, or designate some ecologically-correct meadow areas, but actually what it needs is nothing; it already has the best artwork in the garden – an incredibly heavy, riven oak fence. Plas yn Rhiw needs (and, broadly, has) an owner and a gardener content to see the place run gently, slightly on the back foot, keeping the place in hand but not too smartened up, somewhere the gardener is not licensed to run amok with fashionable exotic planting to increase visitor numbers. Why not do that, you say? Why not attempt an Overbecks (Cornwall) for Wales? Because Plas yn Rhiw already has a telling style of its own, and today, where the generalising influence of fashion is so pervasive, distinction is worth the world.

Gardened ruins are typical of many
a Welsh garden.

A zigzag alley of rock and ferns.

Powis Castle

Welshpool, mid Wales

'Britain has nothing else quite like it'

Powis Castle and its terraces – almost like a reflection in water.

Powis Castle is one of Britain's most memorable gardens. Like Bodnant, everybody has heard of it. But whereas the abiding impression of Bodnant is of looking outwards across the terraces to the mountains, what lingers at Powis, unusually, is an inward prospect, towards that rosy-red castle, perched high upon its marvellous, improbable clouds of clipped yew, and its gorgeously planted terraces below. Britain has nothing else quite like it.

The garden began life in the 1680s with a steeply descending series of Italianate terraces set upon the rocky hillside below the castle; at the bottom, on an open area of levelled ground, were formal water gardens in the Dutch style, with fountains and statuary. Miraculously, the terraces have survived the emulsion brush of fashion, just as did the early eighteenth-century formal garden at Erddig.

In 1771 the landscaper William Eames was employed by the 1st Earl of Powis (Eames also worked at Erddig) to make his more naturalistic additions to the landscape. It was he who planted the wooded wilderness ridge across the little valley from the castle, but he left the older garden intact, perhaps because of the suitability of the existing terraces to the steep terrain. By 1809, however, the need to economise had wiped away the water garden below the terraces to leave an empty space.

A hundred years later the garden was developed again by Lady Violet, wife of the 4th Earl. Not content with the narrow terraces and the wilderness's gilding of rhododendrons, she must have flowers, circulating space and domestic elegance. Below the terraces and behind a line of tall elms lay the walled kitchen garden, and this Lady Violet commandeered to house her new formal gardens. The greenhouses were relocated and in came pretty Edwardian gardening.

Finally, in 1952, Powis passed to the National Trust which made substantial developments to the planting on the terraces, some of it under the then gardens adviser and renowned plantsman, Graham Stuart Thomas. More recently, to reflect current ecological concerns, a wild garden is being developed, where common spotted orchids by the hundreds spangle the grass.

Today you can stand on the terraces at Powis and hear, as you can at Erddig, the whisper of distant traffic – time's wingèd chariot drawing perilously near. Such is the threat to gardens even moderately close to historic towns today, even in rural Wales; how much more this should make us value the absolute silence found in gardens like Dyffryn Fernant and Nant yr Eryd.

The castle through maple foliage.

The garden at Powis plays many a game. Around Lady Violet's formal garden are bold borders, one a superb parade of delphiniums and hollyhocks, some as tall as 13ft and totally free of debilitating rust disease. There's an avenue of hundred year-old, pyramid-trained apples, underplanted with perfect Parks Department circles of golden marjoram or lamb's lugs, and vine tunnels leading to a shady alcove. The last formal enclosure is a pool garden, focused on a grand basin with a central fountain. But by this time the garden has run out of steam; there is too little happening in here. These are open spaces waiting for something to happen, for people to dress the large spaces, and the quality of the gardening around the edge cannot redress that. Visitors drift in and quickly out again.

The seventeenth-century terraces below the castle remain Powis's *pièce de résistance*, even if several of the lesser, intermediate terraces have been put down to grass. First, at the top, comes a great bank of architectural and hot-coloured tropical plants – cannas, bananas, Tetrapanax, angel's trumpets and more. In the terrace wall, elegant niches contain cascading Baroque arrangements of summer bedding, each vase cleverly drilled from below to allow for invisible irrigation pipes.

Opposite: **The Powis coat of arms and fountain in the formal garden.**

Above: **Macleaya x kewensis, Cicerbita alpina and Hydrangea arborescens 'Annabelle'.**

Left: **Fuchsia 'Mary', Lobelia richardsonii, Verbena canadensis, Tropaeolum majus 'Hermine Grasshof'.**

Lady Violet's formal garden sits down below, created over the previous walled garden.

The view from the balustrade is phenomenal; first to the distant hills, second to Eames's wooded wilderness ridge in the middle ground, third down to Lady Violet's formal garden (which, it could be argued, might be usefully hidden behind a new line of trees to leave the distinctiveness of the terraces unmuddied), fourthly onto the empty great lawn where once the water garden lay, and fifthly, on to the borders decorating the terraces immediately below. It is amazing. But turn around and you have the sixth wonder of Powis – the great tumps of clipped yew under the castle walls, looking uncertain whether to prop it up or roll down the hill.

The clipping of the yew fascinates everybody, particularly the vast, buckling hedge beyond Van Nost's statue of Hercules. At Powis it can take four men as long as three months to work round all the yew. Modern machinery helps a great deal, and today there are cherry pickers available which will lift a man way up high from an implausibly narrow base. Scary, but so much better than ladders. Only since 2000 has modern machinery been seriously used at Powis and, with the creation of the necessary gaps in hedges and ramps, it has saved huge amounts of time. The largest pieces of yew at Powis were originally topiary accents of the original 1680s garden and now, after several periods of more informal maintenance, they are sleeping behemoths gathered against the hillside, shapes whose surface texture is as compelling as their outline. They are quite unique in British gardens.

The lower terraces are home to an arched aviary where tender ferns are grown under a dripping canopy of creeping fig, and there's an orangery from which pots of Seville oranges are rolled out each summer. Richly colourful, sophisticated herbaceous borders run left and right of the central steps, and their effect can be scrutinised even from the terrace above; a gardener has to work so hard to pull this off.

Opposite: **Seat cut into a yew tree. Four terraces and the daddy of all yew hedges.**

Left: **The orangery terrace from above.**

Above: **Tetrapanax spreads its wings on the upper terrace over Persicaria microcephala 'Red Dragon' and Salvia 'Indigo Spires'.**

The glories of the terraces.

The arches of the aviary, standing on top of the orangery.

Below these terraces of full-tilt gardening, Powis runs into trouble again. What once was the last three narrower terraces is now a rough grass bank studded prettily with primroses and narcissi over which grows a scattered, motley collection of trees and shrubs for autumn colour, many now diseased. It is difficult to mow and it makes a scruffy, inadequate plinth to the grand picture of the castle and terraces above it (imagine a Christmas cake sitting in a plate of stew and you get the picture). The same lack of substance and *raison d'être* shows in the empty Great Lawn where once the water garden stood. It is a void with no productive relationship to the castle above. How positive it would be now, to pull out all the trees and shrubs on the bank and develop a mass of yews there, even bolder than those which have developed under the castle itself, and to make a grass parterre of the great lawn (mowing patterns of different lengths) as a simple nod to the lost water gardens.

The National Trust has already spelt out the date of its centenary and 'Croeso' in mowing patterns, but something a little more aesthetic than celebratory would work wonders, perhaps drawn, even, from an annual competition. Stand on the wilderness ridge, looking back to the castle, (pictured below) and see what you think.

Do you not have to be standing *on* those terraces for them to look their best today?

The castle and terraces set upon its base of dazzling but spotty trees and shrubs, and the flat lawn where the water garden used to be.

Tony Ridler's Garden

Swansea, south Wales

'Picturesque in the way it follows the philosophy of painters like Ben Nicholson and Mark Rothko'

A permanent architectural planting of box and black phormium in a large metal-lipped planter.

'it's an uncommon location for a garden of this quality'

Over the past twenty years Tony Ridler has made one of the most extraordinary gardens in Wales. Set in a dog-leg behind his very modest terraced house, it covers only a third of an acre, and Ridler has shut out the dull suburban housing which surrounds it to create a very particular secluded world; it's an uncommon location for a garden of this quality, especially in a country where there are so many houses with desirable views where one might make a garden.

Above: **The studio seen through a roof of topiarised ash trees.**

Right: **Emergency sculpture 'Angel Raziel' by David England, provides a focus where a tree came down.**

Ridler, a graphic designer, was born in Swansea, but he thinks of himself primarily as British. He doesn't mind the difficult clay soil and wet climate: "I like the wet," he says, in his calm but enthusiastic voice, "I like it leaden, I like stillness, quiet, nothing going on." But don't think it's a dull garden. Far from it; it's just deceptively simple and endlessly refined. Ask Ridler if he visits many gardens and the answer is no, but that's not to say he is not influenced by what he sees; he admires with a passion, for instance, the ancient, sculptural, espaliered apples in the walled garden at Llanachaeron near Aberystwyth. "A garden needs crispness to make sense," he insists.

Top and left: **Looking two different ways from the same planted tub. In the upper picture, two unseen paths cross the narrow vista.**

You might say it's a garden without a house, for it began life simply to provide an approach to his office in the garden, to make it more interesting for his clients. Like his designs, it would be modern, clean and simple. "There is so much you can do well with only four or five plants," he announces, "It's like fonts in graphic design: there are hundreds of them but you only really need a handful." Is his garden Minimalist, then? "No, it's still cluttered," he insists, "everything should come out that has no reason."

The garden is a most careful composition. If the great Picturesque gardens of the past set out to make pictures imitating the Italian Renaissance landscape paintings of Claude and Poussin, Ridler's garden is Picturesque in the way it follows the philosophy of painters like Ben Nicholson and Mark Rothko, making satisfying compositions of volume, space, line and texture. It is this love of reasonableness that made Ridler such a fan of Sir Roy Strong's books on small gardens, and to admire the Laskett, Strong's thoughtful although infinitely fussier garden in Herefordshire.

The Ridler garden is a series of formal vistas and spaces, largely defined by shallow steps, paths, sculptures and clipped evergreen hedges of box and yew. The openings in the hedges are often only wide enough for one person to squeeze through; it's very much a personal, one-man garden, not a place for exploring side by side while you chat about the planting. Sometimes the path will cut across a vista you have already seen, sometimes more than once, letting you look back to where you started.

Left to right: **Three views moving up the same vista, showing the emerging detail. Note the narrow entrances and topiarised roof of ash trees.**

Opposite: **Ammonite sculpture by Darren Yeadon.**

'there is so much you can do well with only four or five plants'

Please do not walk on the flowers:
a 'paved' waist-high planter launches
the view into another compartment.

But what sets apart the Ridler garden is this: most Classical formal gardens rely on symmetry and perfect balance to bring elegance to a formal space or vista. Tony Ridler, on the other hand, often adopts the centre line of a symmetrical vista, but then proceeds to have not perfect symmetry but varied volumes and spaces on either side of the line, a block of clipped box here, a group of hostas there, which still by their shape and size produce a balanced picture, but dispel the headlong pressure of the truly symmetrical vista. Even with a focal piece of sculpture at the end, Ridler's vistas are modest, cool and unhurried. In a garden as small as this they feel comfortable and relaxed. Of course, creating balance through asymmetry is not an easy thing to do, it requires a great eye; but Ridler has it. "Symmetry's easy," he scoffs.

It's not a garden short of colour. Great swags of rambler roses wrap the scene, and hostas, grasses and clematis, magnolias and a handkerchief tree all help to soften the architecture. There is a whole compartment of luscious hybrid hellebores. In the vegetable garden (yes, there is one) scarlet runner beans, golden marjoram and dramatic cabbages do the same job.

Balance through asymmetry.
Right: **A handkerchief tree.**

Topiary is a major part of the garden, some of it growing in the ground, some of it in containers (including 22 rather abstract chickens), some of it forming a 'flat roof' of ash trees poised over a deck. A score of box bumps, of the especially slow-growing variety 'Morris Minor', have only grown a foot in as many years, which might help Ridler steer clear of RSI and clipper's elbow. Ridler loves his topiary, and the discipline of it; "The more often you do it, the better it gets," he says, and he's right.

Above: **A topiary piece develops a new annexe.**

Centre: **Cloud-pruned box with skimmia below, and Ridler's black walls.**

Above: **The vegetable garden, with apple and fig trees, herbs and bean pyramids.**

Above: **Asymmetry again, leading to the bronze rubbing stone and rambler rose.**

Top right: **'Morris Minor' rally parked amongst the pyramids.**

This is a garden of variation rather than variety: hedges in subtly different colours and heights; paths sticking to the same small palette of materials – old timber from Swansea docks, granite setts, stone and brick – but varying in pattern to suit the moment and the rhythm of the space; a small number of boldly-used containers, lipped with jagged zinc, contain strong effects, from cloud-pruned box to a flat plane of granite setts.

It would be easy to think the garden is too fixed, that apart from clipping there is nothing to do. In fact Ridler is always changing chunks of hedge or topiary that you or I might feel too sacrosanct to alter. For him, form is everything, and he likes to play with it, to adjust, refine. He doesn't invariably get it right, of course. Behind the office is a paved yard surrounded by rendered, black-painted walls, and within it are small, cowed pieces of topiary standing around as if awaiting the call to execution. Ridler needs to fix this and he knows it. Sometimes an area will defeat him and he'll let the maintenance go for a year.

For all its restraint and cool, it's actually a very light-spirited garden, never heavy, and pieces of *trompe l'oeil* on the walls bring a touch of humour. It is in fact fun, like the garden of Ridler's hero Sir Roy Strong. The two of them should get together; they have a lot in common.

Opposite below right: **Dutch tulip fields.**

Left: **A touch of Provence.**

The Dingle

Welshpool, mid Wales

'what an unexpected gem it is,
tucked up a lane outside Welshpool'

**A gravel path zigzags its way up the
gold and silver bank.**

'there is a good, easy-going feel to the place'

Although the Dingle is only a few miles up the road from Powis Castle, it gets only 2–3,000 visitors a year compared to Powis's 102,000. It's a pity because, although the Dingle is not grand or even sophisticated, it is a remarkable twentieth-century period piece with a great deal to teach any gardener.

It began life in 1968 under the hand of nurseryman Roy Joseph and his wife Barbie. She was the gardener and, until her death in 2003, it was very much her baby and planted and cared for by her, although it was open to people visiting their adjoining nursery.

Over the years the nursery prospered despite its remote position (you cannot be more remote than Dibleys houseplant nursery near Ruthin (see page 255), yet it has become one of Wales's great horticultural success stories). Today the nursery covers 150 acres, selling principally to the trade and supplying its own garden centre at Derwen. But the nursery at the Dingle remains extraordinary. It has a catholic list of plants for sale, the like of which one rarely finds today, and gardeners travel long distances to choose from its splendid ranges of trees, shrubs and perennials. What an unexpected gem it is, tucked up a lane outside Welshpool.

Today the garden is entirely separate from the nursery and belongs to Barbie's grandson Duncan and his wife, but they still open it to the public, both of them novices to gardening and picking it up as they go along. It would be nice to think they will manage it. Only a 'Private' sign halfway down the lawn, or sometimes a line of family washing, separates their own space from the visited area and there is a good, easy-going feel to the place.

When the garden began in the 1970s it had all the hallmarks of its day, particularly heathers and conifers (which have now gone), but it still retains that feel of a 1970s-1980s collector's garden, a garden where every must-have tree or shrub has to be tried (a condition aggravated no doubt by having such a good nursery of their own). The result is a very shrub-heavy garden for, as the shrubs developed they were given precedence over any herbaceous planting around their feet; now the more fulsome areas of herbaceous planting only exist around the house lawn and the margins of the pond. It is an uncommon style of garden in a time when perennials and billowing grasses are so fashionable.

A silver-green shrubbery adjoining the house.

That said, the garden does not lack for colour. In spring the far shore of the pond is yellow with self-seeding primroses and later on there are hundreds of flowering trees and shrubs and the new foliage of blue and brown-leaved rhododendrons. In midsummer hydrangeas, hostas, astilbes, crocosmias and day-lilies take over until the great season of autumn colour begins. When people's appetites have been whetted by the garden, the nursery cannot have enough of Trillium grandiflorum, willow gentians and the pale-barked Eucalyptus niphophila.

It's a valley garden, beginning with a level lawn before the house, giving way to a hillside of paths snaking amongst trees and shrubs until they reach the pond in the valley floor. A circular walk runs around the pond and, beyond it, is a woodland garden. The pond was made in the 1950s as a swimming pool, Roy Joseph having offered his children the choice of a television or a pool. Other than that, the garden has not involved much earth-moving and the slope is largely unterraced; paths run diagonally down the slope and only one runs directly across, with a balustrade-like box hedge on the low side to stop it feeling precipitous.

Eucalyptus trunks are reflected in the pond.

Above: **Looking through pines on the north side to the pond.**

Left: **The copper trunk of Prunus serrula.**

**The pond, from side to side. Many of
the trees' foliage is both evergreen and
golden or blue.**

Above: **Clipped cotoneaster separates two paths, with white-stemmed Betula jacquemontii standing beyond.**

Pampas grass doubles in value by water.

It is the planting on the slope that makes the Dingle such an extraordinary place. The lake shore is fringed with grasses, gunneras phormiums and bamboo, and from down here you can look back at the slope and wonder at its planting of trees and shrubs, which dazzles not because of its subtlety but because so much of the foliage is yellow and purple and silver. If it's not your cup of tea, prepare to be dazzled.

Never was there such a panoply of gold, even at Cae Hir: golden yews, pittosporums, escallonias, gleditsias, cypresses, smoke bushes and dozens more. Intermingled with them are purple beechs, maples, hazel, pittosporums, berberis and phormiums. But as your eyes rise up the slope the purple half of the partnership gives way to silver, from olearia, elaeagnus, teucrium, pear, hebe – the list goes on and on – a catalogue of brightness and variegation. Idiosyncratic is what one must call it.

Left: **A dense planting of trees and shrubs means serious thinning must take place.**

Right clockwise from top left:
Euonymus, Viburnum, Parrotia, Prunus serrula bark, Viburnum, Cotinus.

'in this woodland garden the final battle is about to commence'

Beyond the water, the woodland garden is punctuated by secluded wooden shelters with no particular view, in which to pause and rest. Every plant is here, too: magnolias, a handkerchief tree, ironwoods, unusual thorns, maples, azaleas, American oaks, Stewartia and Styrax, and conifers from Podocarpus and Juniperus coxii to the weeping spruce Picea breweriana (the tree universally known to young horticultural students as 'brewer's droop'). The soil is generally bare below, and slate-chip paths make for clean walking, although suddenly there may be an unexpected outbreak of lemon Primula florindae in a damp gulley, or a seeding patch of pale helleborine orchids. It is effectively a small-scale arboretum.

Right: **Japanese maple in all its autumn plumage.**

Opposite: **Golden shrubs cover the bank.**

Far right: **A shelter beyond the pond.**

Like most gardeners, and especially collector-gardeners, Barbie Joseph planted too closely, and when those plants are trees and shrubs then a battle begins, in which the gardener must be arbitrator or the winning plants take all, and the losers die of shade and drought or live on disfigured. In this woodland garden the final battle is about to commence. Duncan Joseph must learn fast and undertake some brave, radical thinning if the garden is to survive. There must be sacrifices of young and old, rare and common, if a healthy community is to thrive in the long term. Keep your eyes high when you visit this garden, and think what you would do. It's a tough call.

The Dingle **223**

The Veddw

Monmouthshire, south east Wales

'the garden always avoids prettiness in favour
of simplicity and cool reasonableness'

**Genista aetnensis and clipped osmanthus
in the front garden.**

The expression 'cottage garden' provokes such different reactions in different people. Many garden lovers smile and say 'Aaaw!' and envisage little old ladies dead-heading amongst pastel roses and hollyhocks; other gardeners bristle at having their life's work labelled as cottage gardening. They take it as an insult, sentimental, trivialising, like calling War and Peace a novella.

Well, The Veddw is a cottage and it's the home of Charles Hawes and his wife Anne Wareham, and they groan angrily if you call it a cottage garden. It's their baby and they won't have it. They prefer it to be called a 'contemporary romantic garden', and certainly it's both of those things. Not that a cottage garden can't be romantic, although it's usually sentimental and with little more to say for itself than loveliness and pretty flowers.

The Veddw has plenty to say for itself. It is a deeply personal project for Wareham and Hawes, and everything in it has been the subject of pleasurably agonising discussion before it came about. There is nothing they like more than to argue about the garden (and everybody else's, come to that) with anyone who's game, and their website is a mine of provocation on the subject of gardens.

Despite facing north across green farmland, it's broadly speaking an inward-looking garden rooted in the soil and in the history of the place. In a wild, romantic bank of montbretia and willow herb, for instance, is a series of beautifully-inscribed grave stones celebrating long-gone local place names. Such things bring you up short, stop you wallowing. A bench higher up the garden is decorated with different spellings of Veddw that have been used down the centuries, as time and political history made their claims upon society. On the slope below the bench is an irregular pattern of chunky box hedges, each space filled with ornamental or crop grasses, in the manner of an agricultural field system. Beyond it – the garden's only compelling long-distance view – is the real field system of the valley, and it makes a remarkable and delightful juxtaposition. Rarely is a garden quite so actively and constructively tied to its landscape.

A 'field system' of clipped box and various ornamental grasses echoes the full-size trees and fields in the landscape beyond.

The garden's core is a series of yew-hedged rooms, clunked together like dice thrown into a gulley. The entrance of one room is made deliberately difficult to find, despite broadcasting a trickle of water, other rooms are simple antechambers or corridors. Most powerful is the zigzag descent through crisp waves of hedging to the reflecting pool and pink, wave-form bench. Some people find sitting here and seeing the bowl of trees and sky reflected in the black-dyed water a serene experience, distilled calm. Some find it most attractively grim, more *Silence of the Lambs* than silence.

Far left top: **Memorial to local place names.**

Far left below: **Seat with different spellings of the area.**

Left: **One of many contrasts of rectilinear and curvilinear formality.**

Above: **Much of the planting has an easy-going, semi-wild feel to it.**

Pink wave-form walls and benches are a recurring motif of the garden and curiously shocking in such a green, deep-rural context. They are compelling, not pretty; almost sexy but tough and linear too. The garden always avoids prettiness in favour of simplicity and cool reasonableness. It can be observed in the 'invisible' black conservatory attached to the house and in the wonderful, jagged black fence staking the garden's claim against the green pasture beyond. Black forms an excellent foil for things which need to stand out, such as the gold lettering on gates and rails (it is used on whole walls in Tony Ridler's garden, p. 208); but black paint becomes perverse, if novel, on prominent benches and steps – objects that are themselves focal.

Opposite: **Water dyed black, and endless dark waves beyond. Abandon hope, all ye who enter here.** Left: **Reaching the pool through the wave hedges, one meets the pink bench, an idealised and perfect version of all the other wave hedges and seats in the garden.** Above: **The seat is made simply of high-quality blockwork and render, painted.**

Occasionally there is a piece of sculpture (discounting for a moment the benches and lettering) in the form of wooden cut-out birds and a stainless-steel water feature, and although they provide important focal points, many people find them unnecessary and a little crude. Nothing would be lost (except vitally, of course, a stroke of the garden's personality) if they disappeared and were replaced with something simpler, perhaps with plants of a powerful form.

There is a woodland of old beech, hornbeam and oak, and again this has a dressing of ideas rather than horticulture; enigmatic inscriptions hung about trees, a lonely wooden chair facing a cloudy-eyed television. There have been attempts at introducing woodland garden plants but they have almost all failed, perhaps for the better: it strengthens the way the wood's simplicity contrasts with the garden proper. There is a tiny ruined cottage too, so frequent in Welsh gardens, which is being turned into a viewing platform complete with a pink-wave wall, from which to see over the garden. Life returns here; but it's also another case of ornamental gardening creeping upon the less-cultivated landscape. How long will the wood hold out?

Opposite: **A jagged, wooden fence, painted black, brings echoes of traditional, Welsh fencing made from long slates set on end.**

Below: **Black wall, black bench, grey-green lyme grass silvered with frost.**

All this makes for a wonderfully provocative, fascinating garden, of which kind there are all too few in Britain. It has guts. But whether Hawes and Wareham like it or not, it's also pretty and even cottagey in places. Behind the house is a semicircular lawn backed by a pleasant enough mixed border, but at the front is a wholehearted, geometric cottage garden with box balls, bird bath, cleverly-used perennials spilling onto gravel paths, roses and clematis on rustic trellis – the works. Admittedly it's not cosy and although its superbly done there is a certain coolness about it. Bizarrely, cars drive in right past the front door, detaching this front garden from the house (why do garden makers never see the value of using a landscape architect to fix such mechanical issues first). It's as if this unowned cottage garden has to be got through before the real fun starts on the other side of a monumental hornbeam archway.

Opposite top: **Semicircular lawn and border behind the house, with Alchemilla mollis, catmint and Epilobium angustifolium 'Stahl Rose'.**

Opposite: **Genista aetnensis and hornbeam arch in the front garden.**

Above: **Euphorbia griffithii glows amongst the black foliage of Lysimachia 'Firecracker' in the front garden.**

And it does. An avenue of lollipop Turkish hazels runs down through a breathtaking meadow of fritillaries, narcissi, wild orchids and camassias, and all around are apples and tree-tops full of honeysuckle and rambling roses filling the air. Clouds of sweet perfume arise from silver Elaeagnus 'Quicksilver' and, with a ventriloquist's flourish, precipitate in distant parts of the garden.

Beyond the meadow is a large potager, now given over to a more ornamental planting of massed artichokes and Heuchera 'Palace Purple'. It's a common fate of potagers (see Lower House, p.102), so many of which sprang into life in the 1980s in the wake of Rosemary Verey's iconic potager at Barnsley House, Gloucestershire. There's no doubt that seeing this one lifts the heart but perhaps a return to formality here, after the 'wild' meadow, is a geometry too far. What's the betting that, in a few years, it becomes another piece of 'ideas gardening'.

There's no guessing which visitor will like The Veddw. Serious gardeners are enthralled, and it is beginning to have small cult following. Other people find it puzzling – not short of flowers but too personal and uncompromising. But never mind liking and disliking; its intellectual ambitions so closely tied to its location make it one of the most interesting gardens in Britain, and a first for Wales.

Fragrant Elaeagnus 'Quicksilver' stands behind the meadow.

Box domes, grey artichokes and
Heuchera 'Palace Purple' in the potager.

Wyndcliffe Court

Chepstow, south east Wales

'what a wonderful example of an Arts and Crafts garden, and what a masterclass its few acres offer to anyone creating any garden at all'

A romantic old garden, nodding but not quite asleep.

At first glance Wyndcliffe Court might seem a weary old place. The substantial red sandstone house was built for Henry Avray Tipping in 1922, in the Arts and Crafts style. It sits comfortable and solid on a hill above Chepstow Racecourse, looking out towards the Bristol Channel and England. Undoubtedly it has seen better days; the house is now subdivided and let, and the garden soldiers on with too little maintenance. But what a garden! What a sweet, neat, gem of a place it is, what a wonderful example of an Arts and Crafts garden, and what a masterclass its few acres offer to anyone creating any garden at all. The more you walk and wander and turn and look again, the better it gets.

Tipping was the architectural editor of *Country Life* magazine, that great promoter of Arts and Crafts houses and gardens, and in whose pages the work of that great English architect and garden designer Edwin Lutyens first appeared. Tipping designed several gardens in Monmouthshire, including, for himself, Wyndcliffe Court and High Glanau (see p. 253).

View out to the river Severn.

Neither house is vast. They are in effect generous country villas, with a few bedrooms, servants' quarters, garages and ancillary buildings. Both occupy high positions with fine views and both have a thoroughly domestic feel, the kind of place one could move into tomorrow. In that wonderful Arts and Crafts manner, the garden is focused firmly on the house; generous, elegant, but nowhere beyond the bounds of necessity for good living.

Left: **Screen gateway from the service entrance.**

Above: **The house is nicely nestled but not smothered in roses.**

Today Wyndcliffe stands at a cross roads. For the last 50 years it was lovingly occupied by Patrick and Betty Clay. Mrs Clay planted her own generation of shrubs and perennials over the bones of Tipping's formal garden, but also in her time the views began to disappear behind shelter-belt trees to the south west, put there to keep out the blasting winds coming off the estuary. Some were planted by Tipping and others are conifers planted since. Tipping's system of informal pools and woodland paths have also been smothered under the shelter planting. But no matter: the rest of the garden on its own is a huge pleasure

and most satisfactory. Like many a Welsh garden with a fine prospect (Bodnant, Powis, Bodysgallen, Plas yn Rhiw) the garden is terraced; firstly a paved sitting terrace where the house walls are covered in Rosa 'Perle d'Or' and banksiae 'Lutea' and there are at least glimpsed views to the Severn and its great bridges; then steps down to a second terrace of simple geometric beds, topiary, and a circular basin fed by a spouting dolphin (in the exact manner of Lutyens's basins at Hestercombe in Somerset); then down again to a long transverse lawn – the bowling alley.

Left: **The second terrace, of topiary and small flower beds.**

Above left: **So much topiary makes a constant opportunity for contrastingly soft planting.**

Above: **One grass allée changes the garden's idiom from curving to rectangular finials.**

Lily basin on the second terrace,
so like the ones at Hestercombe.

Wild and cultivated azaleas mark the change from formal to woodland garden.

To the right is a rectangular sunk garden of stepped borders moving downwards to a rectangular lawn at whose centre is a small lily pool (one might compare the sunk garden at Great Dixter, designed by Nathaniel Lloyd). Nothing is grand, nothing too spacious. And today nothing in too good order either, but you see its intentions.

The sunk garden and upper storey of the ever-present gazebo.

Beside the sunk garden is a pair of parallel mixed borders running down to a pair of iron tracery gates in the kitchen garden wall; but the borders continue all the way through the kitchen garden to gates on the far wall; quite a spectacle. Apart from these borders, the kitchen garden itself now has only apple trees, a few tired borders and the remains of a vine house, peach house, and a melon pit. Spring is the time to see the long borders, still tottering on, for their many oriental poppies, azaleas, paeonies and, later, day lilies and agapanthus.

The elements of Wyndcliffe, therefore, are simple: the terraces, the sunk flower garden and the long borders, with the occasional appearance of water. It's a good, tight arrangement. But there is something else important: an elegant two storey gazebo with a high hipped roof, standing on one corner of the sunk garden. Shades of the Bodnant pin mill, except that here the gazebo is not principally a feature for its own terrace alone: it is the focus for the entire garden, there in the background of every picture, a comforting beacon, a watchtower keeping guard on its provinces and really pulling the garden together. Expensive to build, no doubt, but worth Tipping's every penny (and now desperately in need of someone else's pennies).

The long borders through the walled garden, with Erysimum 'Bowles' Mauve'.

And Wyndcliffe's masterclass? It is in the paths and the paving, something which should be so simple to get right but rarely is so.

First, Wyndcliffe uses only one material throughout – stone – and the fact that it's local stone is a bonus. But it's the way that it's used and styled that is so clever. On the top terrace is the only carved stone – a run of balustrade and ball finials – and thereafter the stonework become progressively less smart and sophisticated, more rustic, until it meets at the garden's field boundaries; the garden works so very closely with its surroundings.

Descending terraces, top to bottom.
Above: **Paving variation on the second terrace.**

Apples under snow.

Thus, the top terrace walls are capped with sawn stone which has had its edges chipped and distressed, just to soften them. The paving here has parallel joints, running outwards from the house to make the terrace seem less long. The steps down are much wider than strictly necessary but so elegant. On the second terrace the paving is in diamond pattern, in some places flanked by crazy paving, and the beds are edged in small upstanding stones. All the steps beyond this point are of good but rough stonework. The long border through the kitchen garden is of gravel, edged, so the plants can comfortably spill forward, with weathered flat rockery stones. Once you become aware of the garden's reducing artificiality, and Tipping's attention to detail, then it is a joy to follow. But does this matter? Well, the garden would be poorer without it, and, most importantly, getting the details right means a garden looks effortlessly good, never mind why. It is just somehow right. Only look at some also-ran Chelsea show gardens, spread with a dog's breakfast of slate chips, flint, gravel, Indian sandstone, concrete slabs, brick, sleepers and decking, and you start to see the high quality and sweet logic of Tipping's work.

Grass bowling alley below the terraces, and gazebo.

Gardens to visit in Wales

Stephen Anderton

Wales has many more gardens than those very special ones featured in this book. Here is a listing, region by region, of these and other gardens you may wish to visit, as well as specialist nurseries and schools of gardening. I offer just a few words of description to tempt you here; they are all interesting to see in their very different ways.

Before visiting any of them, get in touch with the garden to find out about opening dates and times. Details can often be found in the current issue of the *Good Gardens Guide*, the *National Trust Handbook*, and the *Yellow Book* (gardens open for the National Gardens Scheme). Some smaller private gardens are open only occasionally for local charities, or by appointment only, and circumstances change over the years.

South east Wales

1 Dewstow Hidden Gardens and Grottoes
Dewstow House, Caerwent
Monmouthshire NP26 5AH
01291 430444
www.dewstow.com/gardens
Page 64

2 Dyffryn Gardens
St Nicholas, Cardiff,
Vale of Glamorgan CF5 6SU
02920 593328
www.dyffryngardens.org.uk
A garden of large garden rooms, lawns, pools and arboretum, designed by Thomas Mawson for the Reginald Cory in 1906 and now owned by Vale of Glamorgan local government. Since 1997 it has received much needed funds from the Heritage Lottery Fund for restoration. New road, toilets and shop, and repair of garden buildings, but still rough round the edges and some of the middle.

3 High Glanau Manor Garden and Garden School
Lydart, Monmouth NP25 4AD
01600 860005
Like Wyndcliffe Court, another Arts and Crafts garden by Henry Avray Tipping. Under loving restoration.

4 Llanover House & Garden School
Llanover, Abergavenny,
Monmouthshire NP7 9EF
www.llanovergarden.co.uk
An attractive country house garden, with park, circular walled garden and a growing collection of rare trees. Garden lecture series commanding the best speakers.

5 Lower House
Cussop Dingle, Hay on Wye HR3 5RQ
01497 820773
www.lowerhousegardenhay.co.uk
Page 98

6 Arne Maynard Garden Design School, Usk
c/o Arne Maynard Design
2nd Floor, 14 Baltic Street East,
London EC1Y 0UJ
0207 689 8100
Design courses held at the country home of award-winning garden designer Arne Maynard. Productive garden and earth landforms.

7 Penpergwm Lodge Garden and Nursery
Abergavenny, Monmouthshire NP7 9AS
01873 840208
www.penplants.com

A rich and complex country garden, formal and informal, with large pergola, terrace, small avenues and walled garden with rill. Selling plants grown in the garden.

8 St Fagans National History Museum and Castle
St Fagans, Cardiff CF5 6XB
02920 573500
www.museumwales.ac.uk
Open-air National History Museum, with recreated formal and informal gardens including Arts and Crafts Italianate garden, rose garden, arboretum and parterre.

9 Tredegar House
Newport, Gwent NP10 2PD
01633 815880
www.tredegar.house@newport.gov.uk
A 17th century mansion close to the M4 motorway. The grounds include an orangery, a walled garden and an historic parterre filled with coloured gravels. Parkland.

10 The Veddw
Devauden, Monmouthshire NP16 6PH
01291 650836
www.veddw.co.uk
Page 224

11 Whimble Garden and Nursery
Kinnerton, Presteigne, Powys LD8 2PD
01547 560413
www.whimblegardens.co.uk
A modest country garden big on herbs, and having a go with turf-mound work, little used in Wales so far (there is some at Arne Maynard's garden also – see entry 6).

12 Wyndcliffe Court
St Arvans, near Chepstow,
Monmouthshire NP16 6EY
01873 880257
Page 238

South west Wales

13 Aberglasney
Llangathen, Llandeilo,
Carmarthenshire SA32 8QH
01558 668998
www.aberglasney.org
Page 08

14 Cae Hir
Cribyn, Lampeter,
Ceredigion SA48 7NG
01570 470839
www.caehirgardens.ws
Page 52

15 Clyne Gardens
Blackpill, Swansea,
West Glamorgan SA3 5BD
01792 401737
A park more than a garden with woodland walks and pool. Three National Collections, of Rhododendron, Pieris and Enkianthus.

16 Colby Woodland Garden
Amroth, Narberth,
Pembrokeshire SA67 8PP
01834 811885
www.nationaltrust.org.uk
A wooded hillside traversed with paths and underplanted with rhododendrons. There is an ornamental walled garden with mixed borders, summerhouse and rill.

17 Dyffryn Fernant
Llanchaer, Fishguard SA65 9SP
01348 811282
www.genuslocus.net
Page 76

18 Farmyard Nurseries
Llandysul, Carmarthen,
Pembrokeshire SA44 4RL
01559 363389
www.farmyardnurseries.co.uk
Specialising in unusual herbaceous plants with particular collections of hellebores, Tricyrtis and Schizostylis, particularly named garden varieties.

19 Gwynfor Growers
Pontgarreg, near Llangrannog
Llandysul SA44 6AU
01239 654151
www.gwynfor.co.uk
A small organic nursery growing a wide range of shrubs, climbers and herbaceous plants. Good on seaside varieties. Heritage fruit trees including the Welsh 'Bardsey' apple.

20 Hafod
Hafod Trust, Hafod Estate Office,
Pontrhydygroes, Ystrad-Meurig,
Ceredigion SY25 6DX
01974 282568
www.hafod.org
The remains of a once wonderful landscape, still worth seeing for its woodland walks and waterfalls. The house no longer exists. Stout shoes and imagination required.

21 Llanerchaeron
Ciliau Aeron, near Aberaeron,
Ceredigion SA48 8DG
01545 570200
www.nationaltrust.org.uk
A simple country house by Nash with home farm. No ornamental garden to speak of but the colourful, romantic walled garden has huge charm. Fine old espalier apples.

22 Llanllyr
Talsarn, Lampeter, Ceredigion SA48 8QB
01570 470900
A flat valley-bottom garden made on historic bones but with much modern development including deep parallel rose borders. Very sweet, but kitsch in parts.

23 Nant-yr-Eryd
Abercych, Boncath,
Pembrokeshire SA37 0EU
Page 112

24 National Botanic Garden of Wales
Middleton Hall, Llanarthne,
Carmarthenshire SA32 8HG
01558 667132/667134
www.gardenofwales.org.uk
Page 124

25 Pant yr Holiad
Rhydlewis, Llandysul, Ceredigion SA44 5ST
01239 851493
A large garden specialising in species rhododendrons and varieties bred here. Hydrangeas. Secret rose garden, walled garden, pond, potager and scenic walks.

26 Picton Castle and Woodland Gardens
Haverfordwest, Pembrokeshire SA62 4AS
01437 751326
www.pictoncastle.co.uk
Woodland garden with ancient trees, maze, rhododendrons, spring-flowering shrubs and wild flowers. Fern walk. Walled garden with fountain, roses and herbs.

27 Tony Ridler's Garden
7 St Peter's Terrace, Swansea SA2 0FW
01792 582100
Page 200

28 Singleton Botanical Gardens
Singleton Park, Swansea,
West Glamorgan SA2 9DU
01792 298637
www.swansea.gov.uk
A walled garden, with glasshouses for desert, Tropical and Economic plants. Herbaceous borders, herb garden and colourful bedding-out schemes.

29 Slade Garden and Garden School
Southerndown,
Vale of Glamorgan CF32 0RP
01656 880048
A genial seaside garden in a sheltered green gully just set back from the sea shore, most notable for its interesting lecture series held in the house.

North west Wales

30 Aber Artro Hall
Llanbedr, Gwynedd LL45 2PA
01341 241777
An earnest Arts and Crafts hillside garden undergoing serious repair. Imaginative and, some would say, brave new Italian and William Morris (installation) gardens.

31 Aberconwy Nursery
Graig, Glan Conwy, Colwyn Bay
Conwy LL28 5TL
01492 580875
An excellent alpine nursery specialising in saxifrages, autumn gentians, small ferns and dwarf ericaceous plants. Just down the road from Bodnant.

32 Bodnant
Tal-y-Cafn, Colwyn Bay, Conwy LL28 5RE
01492 650460
www.bodnantgarden.co.uk
Page 20

33 Bodrhyddan
Rhuddlan, Denbighshire LL18 5SB
01745 590414
Page 32

34 Bodysgallen Hall (Historic House Hotels)
Llandudno, Gwynedd LL30 1RS
01492 584466
www.bodysgallen.com
Page 42

35 Crûg Farm Plants
Griffith's Crossing, near Caernarfon
Gwynedd LL55 1TU
01248 670232
www.crug-farm.co.uk
This small nursery and even smaller garden are a shrine to serious plant collectors across the world (the owners themselves collect in the wild.) From the green to the gorgeous.

36 Foxbrush
Aber Pwll, Port Dinorwic
Gwynedd LL56 4JZ
01248 670463
Small riverside garden, best in spring, with ponds, bridges, laburnum tunnel, long rose pergola and herbaceous borders. Unusual and much-treasured plants throughout.

37 Maenan Hall
Llanrwst, Conwy LL26 0UL
01492 640441
A heavy-duty country house garden, rather like an offshoot of Bodnant (it belongs to the same family) with plenty of rhododendrons and roses, and a dell garden.

38 Penrhyn Castle
Bangor, Gwynedd LL57 4HN
01248 371337
www.nationaltrust.org.uk
Pleasant parkland around a nineteenth-century Norman castle, and new woodland garden; the star is the walled garden with early twentieth-century terraces and a fuchsia tunnel.

39 Plas Brondanw
Llanfrothen, Penrhyndeudraeth
Gwynedd LL48 6SW
07880 766741
www.brondanw.org
Page 138

40 Plas Cadnant
Cadnant Road, Menai Bridge
Anglesey LL59 5NH
01248 717007
www.plascadnant.co.uk
Page 148

41 Plas Newydd
Llanfairpwll, Anglesey LL61 6DQ
01248 715272
www.nationaltrust.org.uk
Page 160

42 Plas yn Rhiw
Rhiw, Pwllheli, Gwynedd LL53 8AB
01758 780219
www.nationaltrust.org.uk
Page 174

43 Portmeirion
Minffordd, Penrhyndendraeth
Gwynedd LL48 6ER
01766 770000
www.portmeirion-village.com
A woodland garden with flowering trees and shrubs and some huge specimens. Amongst the village buildings are seasidey patches of public planting.

44 Rickards Ferns
Lon Rallt, Pentir, Bangor,
Gwynedd LL57 4RP
01248 600385
www.rickardsferns.co.uk
Not much to see, but heaven if you like ferns. Natives, exotics and fancy forms. Available at the usual garden centre sizes, but also – for a price – much larger.

North east Wales

45 Banwy Valley Nursery
Llangadfan, near Welshpool, Powys SY21 0PT
01938 820281
www.banwnursery.co.uk
Tucked away up a hair-raisingly (to some) narrow road, it is a bit scruffy but full of wonderful plants you would never expect to find in mid Wales. Always worth a look.

46 Celyn Vale Eucalyptus Nurseries

Carrog, Corwen, Merioneth LL21 9LD
01490 430671
www.eucalyptus.co.uk
Who said eucalyptus are all huge and only live in a dry climate! The best place in the UK to buy eucalyptus species of all sizes, with an excellently informative website.

47 Dibley's Nurseries and Arboretum

Llanelidan, Ruthin, Denbighshire LL15 2LG
01978 790677
www.dibleys.com
A successful grower of house plants, with vast glasshouses stuck implausibly up a hilltop. There is a sizeable modern arboretum, ornamental rather than scientific.

48 The Dingle Garden and Nursery

Welshpool, Powys SY21 9JD
01938 555145
www.dinglenurseries.co.uk
Page 212

49 Donadea Lodge

Mynydd Llan, Babell, Holywell
Clwyd CH8 8QD
01352 720204
A small shady garden, offering ideas about what can be grown there, especially using different colour schemes. Specialising in clematis.

50 Chirk Castle

Chirk, Wrexham LL14 5AF
01691 777701
www.nationaltrust.org
A 700-year-old castle, now a mansion with wonderful old clipped yew hedges. Views, remarkable rustic summerhouse and some flower borders.

51 Erddig

Wrexham, Clwyd LL13 0YT
01978 355314
www.nationaltrust.org
Page 86

52 The Garden House

Erbistock, Wrexham LL13 0DL
01978 781149
www.simonwingett.com
A richly planted modern garden and hydrangea collection (also for sale). Sculpture throughout the garden's many modern and traditional garden rooms. Still expanding.

53 Glansevern Hall

Berriew, Welshpool
Powys SY21 8AH
01686 640644
www.glansevern.co.uk
Greek Revival house leading to a lake surrounded by bog and woodland gardening. New rill garden, richly subdivided walled garden, and wood populated by statuettes.

54 Powis Castle

Welshpool, Powys SY21 8RF
01938 551929
www.nationaltrust.org.uk
Page 186

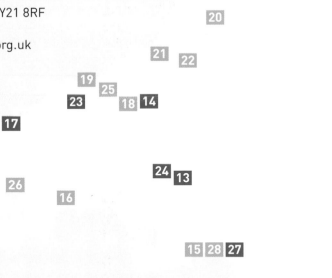

Published by Graffeg
First published 2009
Copyright © Graffeg 2009
ISBN 978 1 905582 20 4

Graffeg, Radnor Court, 256 Cowbridge
Road East, Cardiff, CF5 1GZ, Wales UK.
Tel: +44 (0)29 2037 7312
sales@graffeg.com www.graffeg.com
Graffeg are hereby identified as the authors
of this work in accordance with section 77
of the Copyrights, Designs and Patents
Act 1988.

Distributed by the Welsh Books Council
www.wbc.org.uk castellbrychan@wbc.org.uk

A CIP Catalogue record for this book is
available from the British Library.

Designed and produced by
Peter Gill & Associates
sales@petergill.com
www.petergill.com

Discovering Welsh Gardens is written by
Stephen Anderton with photography
by Charles Hawes. The © copyright of
photographs is attributed to
Charles Hawes.

The publisher acknowledges the financial
support of the Welsh Books Council
www.gwales.com

The author and photographer wish to
acknowledge the help and good will of
the National Trust.

Every effort has been made to ensure that
the information in this book is current and
it is given in good faith at the time of
publication. Please be aware that
circumstances can change and be sure to
check details before visiting any of the
gardens featured.

**Photography and acknowledgements
from Charles Hawes.**

All the photographs for this book were
taken on Fuji Velvia ISO 50, 35mm film.
I'm a bit of a dinosaur in still using film as
most of my colleagues have gone digital.
The writing is on the wall. The vast majority
were taken with Canon EOS3 body, with
either a Canon 24-70 F 2.8L lens or the
Canon 70-200 F 2.8L and the panoramic
format pictures with a Hasselblad XPan
with the 45mm F4 lens.

I would like to thank all the garden
owners and head gardeners for their
co-operation and assistance with my need
to be in the gardens very early in the
morning or until last light and for their
patience with my complaints about the
weather. And for making such wonderful
gardens for us all to enjoy.

One person deserves my thanks beyond
all others. My wife, Anne Wareham, who
brought gardens into my life, made our
garden such a special place and who
encouraged me to take up photographing
gardens.